———————————————————

"IF YOU HOLD TO MY TEACHING, YOU ARE REALLY MY DISCIPLES.
Then you will know the truth, and the
truth will set you free."

JOHN 8:31B, 32

———————————————————

Note for Librarians: A cataloguing record for this book is available from Library and Archives Canada at www.collectionscanada.ca/amicus/index-e.html

ISBN 978-1-4251-1200-4

 www.trafford.com

North America & international
toll-free: 1 888 232 4444 (USA & Canada)
phone: 250 383 6864 ♦ fax: 250 383 6804 ♦ email: info@trafford.com

The United Kingdom & Europe
phone: +44 (0)1865 722 113 ♦ local rate: 0845 230 9601
facsimile: +44 (0)1865 722 868 ♦ email: info.uk@trafford.com

Order this book online at www.trafford.com/06-2959

10 9 8 7 6 5 4 3 2

Uprooting Anger

Destroying the Monster Within

Kay W. Camenisch

Dedication

I would like to dedicate this book to the couples who came to Eagle Springs Training Center in Skiatook, Oklahoma, in 2000 and 2001, seeking help for family strife. Your courage to share your pain and suffering led me on the quest to learn what God had to say about anger. If you had not been brave enough to bare your hearts and souls, this book never would have been started.

Acknowledgments

First of all, I would like to thank the many people who offered encouragement and help. The prayers of Rebecca Camenisch and encouragement of Tricia Lawrence gave birth to the vision of making a book of the things God had shown me. Cec Murphey encouraged me and began my education of the writing and publishing world. And the Grassroots Writers Group offered ongoing encouragement, helping me believe that God could use even me. Assurance and reassurance—from these and numerous others—that God could use me and that the material had merit, kept me going when I would have given up.

After I signed a contract to publish *Uprooting Anger,* I panicked. Then God provided a family with the encouragement and expertise to finish the task. Timus Rees gave counsel and confidence to move forward. Donna saved the day with her expert advice and editing. Their daughter, Becky, was a lifesaver with the layout. I am grateful for the Reeses. They made it happen.

I am especially grateful for my children for their constant encouragement and for their artistic contributions. Specifically, Jonathan graciously and patiently worked with me in the formation of a website, Julia A. and Stephanie served as regular sounding boards and cheerleaders, while Daniel and Julia D. offered counsel and made a video for promotion. My nephew Andrew Camenisch created the book cover, which communicates anger far better than I could imagine. I have been blessed by encouragement from many family members.

I particularly owe thanks to my dear husband, Robert, who encouraged and helped me from the beginning. I didn't believe I could write. Without his support, I never would have recorded what the Lord showed me, and certainly would not have persevered to publication. His wisdom, patience, gentleness, encouragement and generosity of time and funds held me to the task.

My name is on the book as author, but I could never have completed *Uprooting Anger* on my own. I am most indebted to my God. He burdened me with urgency to find answers for anger, gave me insights I had never seen before, and arranged circumstances and encouragement to keep me working. When I put the project back in the file, the Lord would cause something to happen to make me pull it out and work on it some more. When I plowed forward to make things happen, God would block all doors until I gave up—then He would bring it about. *Uprooting Anger* has my name on it, but it is really God's book. I pray that through it, many will find freedom from anger and that the Lord will receive the glory, the honor, and the praise.

Foreword

Confronting anger is painful because it exposes our pride and personal failures. Pride is the sin that God hates the most and punishes the quickest. As a result of pride, Lucifer was forced out of heaven, Adam and Eve were expelled from the Garden of Eden, Moses was not allowed to enter the Promised Land, and countless numbers of people are deprived of the joy and fulfillment of God-given relationships. "Only by pride cometh contention" (Proverbs 13:10).

For this reason, I encourage you to study this book and to cry out to God for His deliverance from the spirit of anger. Crying out to God must be preceded by thanking God for His purposes in allowing trials in our lives and also by fulfilling all the vows that we have made to Him.

"Offer unto God thanksgiving; and pay thy vows unto the most High: And call upon me in the day of trouble: I will deliver thee, and thou shalt glorify me" (Psalm 50:14–15).

Through Christ our Lord,

Bill Gothard

TABLE OF CONTENTS

How to Get the Most Out of This Study

Uprooting Anger: Destroying the Monster Within is for anyone who is tired of trying to cope with, manage, or control anger. It is for those who are ready to work in cooperation with the Holy Spirit to break free from anger's destructive hold. The help received will depend in large part on the diligence given to seeking God's truth and applying it. Below are some suggestions for getting the most out of this study.

Prayer

"Out of the heart flow the issues of life"—including the issue of anger. Therefore, in order to gain lasting freedom from anger, it is necessary to deal with the heart. Since only God can change our hearts, we are dependent on Him. Therefore, prayer is foundational to breaking free. Begin each lesson with prayer, asking the Lord to open your eyes to see, your ears to hear, and your heart to receive the truth He has for you.

Understanding the truths presented will help in recognizing the root of the anger in a particular situation. However, you will never uproot anger with understanding. Therefore, as you study, prayerfully seek the Lord to bring change in your heart through His Word. It is through such transformation that you will increasingly find lasting freedom from anger's bondage.

The Word

The Word of God does not return void; it will accomplish His purposes (Isa. 55:11). Therefore, this book is based on what the Bible says about anger, not on man's observations and insights. Scripture passages are assigned at the beginning of the study to give the background history from which the meditation is written or to give foundational material on the subject that is covered. Reading those passages will increase understanding of the meditation. They also provide a foundation on which to answer the questions in the Application Section.

The key verse for the study is listed immediately above the meditation and is repeated at the beginning of the Application Section.

Meditation

The key verse is the beginning point and the focal point for the meditation that follows. The meditations seek to apply to our lives the truth found in that verse. As you read each one, seek application in your own life. Throughout the day, continue to meditate on the key passage, asking God for additional insight and application.

Prayer

Each meditation closes with a prayer focus, offering guidelines for prayer centered on the truths presented. The prayers are guided, rather than written out, so you can communicate with God in your own words, sharing what is on your heart. Go to Him with the expectation that He wants you to find freedom. Be open and honest; cry out to Him for mercy, forgiveness, and grace.

Application

The Scriptures and the principles presented will bring freedom only as they are applied to your life. As you answer the questions, be open and honest about your own tendencies, shortcomings, and failures. Listen for God's voice as you study His Word. Like so much in life, the more you apply yourself, the more you will gain from the study.

Digging Deeper

Additional Scripture has been added to provide more verses that deal with the topic covered in the lesson. There may not be time to look up every passage every time, but if a lesson deals with an area where you are weak, make time to look up the verses listed. You can be strengthened in the area of struggle by learning more of what God says about it. Feed on the Word, meditate on the Word, and ask God to make it real in your life.

As you dig into the Word, the Lord will give you insights beyond those directly in the study. You will also gain new insights from what others share if you are in a group. Space has been left on each page so you can write them down. As you make note of them, it will help to cement them in your memory and will provide a record of them for use in the future.

The wide margin also can be used to record a summary of the Scripture passages you read, encouraging you to read them more carefully. Then, when you discuss the questions with a group, your notes will be handy.

Our Hope Is in God

Daily look to God for help, "being confident of this very thing, that he which hath begun a good work in you will perform it until the day of Jesus Christ" (Phil. 1:6).

Benefits of Group Study

Using *Uprooting Anger: Destroying the Monster Within* with others will increase your gain from the study. Studying the book with a group will:

* Strengthen each individual as each person knows he is not alone in the battle to overcome anger.

* Provide greater insight and application through discussion and testimonies, as group members pray for one another.

* Encourage accountability as the members check on and report to one another.

* Increase motivation and strength to persevere to the finish.

* Build the body of Christ as the group members learn to be open, honest, and supportive of one another.

Suggestions for Group Leaders

1. Keep the group small enough that individuals can share openly about their struggles.

2. Keep everything shared within the group confidential. Agree ahead of time not to repeat anything that has been shared at the meeting.

3. Open and close each session with prayer. The end of the meeting might be used to break into accountability partners (or threesomes), to share prayer requests, and to pray for each other.

4. Accountability partners could be assigned at each session, giving each participant permission to call the assigned partner between meetings—when struggling with anger or to confess a failure.

5. At the first meeting:

   a. Use the introduction to share the concept that anger has many roots and that the study will address different roots and seek God for redemption.

   b. Establish the need for confidentiality within the group.

   c. Go through the steps on how to use the study in order to familiarize everyone with the format.

   d. Assign lesson one and set the schedule for regular meetings. Encourage everyone to do his/her homework in order to learn, to gain freedom, and to be able contribute to discussion at the next meeting.

6. At subsequent meetings:

   a. Pray.

   b. Discuss the meditation. Let participants share insights gained and answer questions raised.

c. Discuss the Application pages. Every question does not need to be addressed, but principles and concepts from clusters of questions need to be covered to see if there is general understanding or if questions remain. Openness, honesty, and vulnerability by the leader will encourage others to be transparent. Do not judge others or force them to be open. Allow the Holy Spirit to lead.

d. Give opportunity for testimony of how application of the lesson has had an impact—or is needed—in the lives of the participants.

e. If time permits, give opportunity for testimony of how former lessons have strengthened members to overcome anger in the past week.

f. Pray for one another, either taking prayer requests or by breaking into accountability groups.

g. Note that Lesson 4 ("You Choose"), Lesson 11 ("Be Ye Kind"), and Lesson 13 ("Be Not Bitter") are longer than most, with additional application at the end of the study. These are very important additions. Without taking care of these issues, anger will remain. You may want to break these lessons into two sessions in order to be thorough with gaining a clear conscience, forgiving others, and overcoming bitterness.

7. "Digging Deeper" has a list of Scripture passages that will give further insight into topics that will likely arise during discussion of the lesson. If you become familiar with these verses before the meeting, you will be better prepared for discussion that might develop. The verses could also be used as a focal point to initiate further discussion of the topic, or for memory work.

Introduction

Anger is rampant. Like a monster, it is destroying individuals, families, and churches. Unresolved anger breeds more anger and often leads to violence and destruction. Many are terrorized by it. Others are in bondage to it. The harder you try to control it, the more often it erupts. Anger, left unchecked, is sure to grow.

While anger itself is not evil, unresolved anger is not part of God's design for man. God tells us to put anger off, to put it behind us (Ezek. 45:9, Eph. 4:31–32), and to walk in His righteousness. God would not command us to do that if He didn't provide the means to accomplish it. Unfortunately, few gain freedom from their anger.

Anger is like a dandelion. As a weed, it is unwanted. Left unchecked its seeds are carried far and wide, propagating consequences far beyond the source. The seeds of the dandelion sail through the air, landing on unsuspecting soil. Soon, unsightly plants spring forth in lawns, flower beds, and even in the cracks of concrete sidewalks.

Dandelions are difficult to get rid of because their roots extend deep into the soil. It is almost impossible to pull up a dandelion without leaving some of the root in the ground—which will then grow a new plant. You must dig to get to the end of the long taproot, which extends deep into the ground.

Anger and dandelions are similar in the way they spread, but their roots are very different. Dandelion roots are distinctly "dandelion." Unlike the dandelion, the roots of anger are often deep, but they are many— like the roots of a tree—and are not distinctly "anger." Consequently, they are not usually easily identified. People try desperately to pull up the root of anger, but they find themselves still angry because they don't successfully identify the roots.

Pulling up anger is much more difficult than pulling up a dandelion root, because anger grows from many roots. These roots have many identities, including guilt, pride, bitterness, selfishness, fear, desire for control, and many more. In order to rid ourselves of anger, each root that has become deeply anchored in our lives needs to be correctly identified and uprooted.

If our lives are plagued with anger, we need a sure solution—one that will last. The best place to find lasting solutions for problems in our lives is in the Word of God. In *Uprooting Anger: Destroying the Monster Within,* Bible passages that deal with anger are considered in order to identify the roots from which anger grows. Meditations on various verses of Scripture explore truths from God to help us understand what He has to say. In order to fully attack the root that is revealed, with each meditation study pages are included to help make personal application of each truth.

We've heard and gained hope from this verse: "Ye shall know the truth, and the truth shall make you free" (John 8:32). Why, then, do many of us—even though we know the truth—not walk in the freedom that is available to us? Later in the passage, Jesus tells us why: "I know that ye are Abraham's seed [those entrusted with God's Word]; but ye seek to kill me, *because my word hath no place in you*" (John 8:38, italics added). When we know the truth (His Word), but it has no place in us, we are not set free by it. We must apply the truth to our lives, taking it into ourselves. We'll be set free only as completely as the truth is applied in our lives. *Uprooting Anger* will help reveal God's truths concerning anger and will serve as a tool to help us apply those truths to our lives.

I began this study as I sought answers for families whom we were counseling. I was devastated as I saw great destruction in numerous Christian homes—destruction caused by anger. I began to search the Scriptures to find God's answer for victory over anger. I hoped for a quick-fix, one-size-fits-all formula that would bring freedom from the terror and destruction I saw, but the more I looked, the more frustrated I became.

I discovered that the Bible has much to say about anger, but I couldn't find a formula that was common to all the passages. After much frustration, I read just one passage at a time and asked God to speak to me out of His Word. He did, and I was excited about what I learned. I wrote down what He showed me and studied to understand more. The next day I had a similar experience from another passage. And the next day another.

Before I knew it, I had a stack of meditations. I still didn't have the quick-fix solution that I'd hoped for. Instead, I saw that anger doesn't have a simple solution—because it has many roots, and each must be dealt with.

We are often frustrated because we take care of one root and hope that our problem is solved. We don't realize that there are other roots which are continuing to provide nourishment that keeps our anger alive and healthy. When attacking anger, we need to work diligently to "lay aside *every* weight, and the sin which doth so easily beset us, and . . . run with patience the race that is set before us, looking unto Jesus the author and finisher of our faith" (Heb. 12:1b–2a, italics added). We need to persevere, running with patience as we continue pulling up those roots that would cause us to stumble. Without patience and perseverance we will not complete the journey. However, the key to success is to look to Jesus, because He is the author and the finisher of our faith. It is in Him that we can be made into new creatures.

As I looked for answers for others, I quickly realized that I had a problem too. As I had compared my anger to the volatile explosions of some, I had self-righteously concluded that I didn't have a problem because I wasn't as bad as they were. I was maybe more controlled, didn't blow up as loudly or as frequently, and was better at justifying my anger—but my problem was as real as that of those whom I was seeking to help. I also discovered that it wasn't as hidden as I thought it was. Others knew I had a problem with anger whether I knew it or not. I am grateful for this study. God has used it for my own personal growth, not only in overcoming my anger, but also in making me much less judgmental of others who get angry.

I know that God is working in your life, or you wouldn't be reading this book. My prayer is that this would be a tool that God would use to help you uproot anger and to help you grow in your relationship with Him. May the Lord give you grace, strength, and perseverance for the journey.

1 He Is Sufficient!

"Let no corrupt communication proceed out of your mouth, but that which is good to the use of edifying, that it may minister grace unto the hearers. Let all bitterness, and wrath, and anger, and clamor [loud, noisy expressions], and evil speaking, be put away from you, with all malice" (Ephesians 4:29, 31).

Read 2 Corinthians 12:7–10.

God makes it clear that He does not want any expression of anger left in our lives. He wants it all gone, all put away. We are to be without it.

* Bitterness (which grows from anger that is taken inward and held) needs to be put away.

* Wrath (the passion that grips) needs to be put away.

* Anger (the thought and passion that would seek vengeance) needs to be put away.

* Clamor (the outward expression of anger) needs to be put away.

* Evil speaking (the railing and seeking to tear another down) needs to be put away.

* All malice (the evil, wicked thoughts that develop in our hearts and minds when we are angry) needs to be put away.

This could seem overwhelming to anyone who has unsuccessfully battled with anger. However, the Lord gives us hope by telling us that His grace is sufficient (2 Cor. 12:9), and all things are possible through Him (Matt. 19:26, Lk. 18:27). He would not ask this of us if it were something that couldn't happen.

The key is to remember that it is His grace that is sufficient. It is through Him that all things are possible. If we keep our hopes on ourselves and our own efforts, we are doomed. Only as we look to Him for our salvation do we find His grace sufficient.

He Is
Sufficient!

Sometimes after an episode with anger we pray and ask God to free us from it; then we are disappointed in God for not answering our prayer. If we run to Him only in the crisis, only when we have a need, we will never fully tap into the grace that is available.

Our God is a relational God, not a problem solver on call. We grow in grace and strength through an intimate relationship with Him.

Jesus faced the ultimate abuse, and He never lost His temper or spoke a word in His own defense. He was one with His Father and often slipped away for time alone with Him. His strength is available to us. His grace is sufficient. The question is, Are we sufficiently related with Him?

Pray: Confess to the Lord times of depending on your own strength and of seeking God only during the crises. Praise Him for His example of strength under control at Calvary, and tell Him you desire a closer relationship with Him. Ask Him to change your heart and draw you near to Himself.

1 He Is Sufficient!

Application of Ephesians 4:31

"Let all bitterness, and wrath, and anger, and clamor, and evil speaking, be put away from you, with all malice" (Ephesians 4:31).

Read John 15:4–5.

1. What life does the branch have apart from the vine?

   _____

2. What has to happen for the branch to not receive life and strength from the vine? _____

   _____

   _____

3. When (how often, for how long, etc.) is the branch attached to the vine?

   _____

4. How is the branch truly one with the vine? _____

   _____

   _____

   _____

5. What identity does the branch have apart from the vine?

   _____

6. If the branch has to be attached to the vine, stay attached to the vine, and receive its life from the vine, what does that say about your life in Jesus Christ?

   _____

   _____

   _____

7. What can the branch do (what fruit can it produce?) apart from the vine? _____

_____

Read Galatians 5:22–25.

Use each anger event as a signal to spend time with the Lord and draw close to Him.

8. What is the fruit that is produced when we are abiding in the Vine?

_____

_____

_____

9. Can anger co-exist with any of the fruit listed? Why, or why not?

_____

_____

_____

Read Psalm 37:5–6.

10. What are the two verbs that indicate what action you should take?

_____

11. How does the righteousness (the fruit, the conquering of anger) happen? _____

_____

_____

When tensions arise and anger erupts, that is a sign that you are no longer abiding in Him.

Pray: Ask God to help you abide in Him and develop a closer relationship with Him.

Digging Deeper:

John 17:21–23, 26

2 Corinthians 12:9–10

Revelation 3:20

1 Corinthians 7:23–24

Philippians 1:9–11

1 John 1:3–4

1 John 2:28–29

1 Corinthians 1:9

2 Jesus Made a Scourge

"When he [Jesus] had made a scourge [whip] of small cords, he drove them all out of the temple, and the sheep, and the oxen; and poured out the changers' money, and overthrew the tables" (John 2:15).

Read Matthew 21:12–17.

Jesus is our example. He made a scourge, drove the traders and the livestock out of the temple, poured out the money, and overthrew the tables. For the disciples, it brought to mind Psalm 69:9: "The zeal [jealousy] of thine house hath eaten me up." Jesus was driven by zeal to what appears to be a response of fury. If Jesus could get angry, it's permissible for me to get angry. Right? Well, let's look more closely.

Anger is generally a negative reaction rather than a positive action. It is normally re-active, rather than pro-active. However, Jesus did only what His Father told Him to do (see John 5:19 and 30), so we know that Christ's demonstration in the temple was not a reaction to the scene that greeted Him. Instead, it was action carried out in response to His Father.

If we are around someone who has an angry outburst, we want to fight back or to run. How did those around Jesus respond?

* The disciples were reminded of a verse from Psalms (John 2:17).

* The Jews asked for a sign to show what authority He had for doing it (John 2:18).

* The blind and lame came to Him for healing (Matthew 21:14).

* He taught in the temple the rest of the day, and "the chief priests and scribes saw the wonderful things that He did."

* The children cried "Hosanna to the son of David," making the chief priests and scribes indignant (Matthew 21:15).

No one reacted negatively to the "angry" outburst. The chief priests and scribes were the ones under attack. They questioned His authority, but they then allowed Him to heal and teach in the temple.

Could it be that rather than reacting in anger, Jesus was acting under authority? Wasn't He pro-active (taking the initiative to intervene) rather than re-active (acting in opposition)? Could it be that Jesus was taking dominion—dominion that was rightfully His as the Son of God?

If Jesus had cleansed the temple in reactive anger, would the priests have allowed him to teach in the temple the rest of the day? When we become angry, do we respond to God and act as His representative? Or do we react in opposition to what we don't like?

Pray: If you have considered the incident of Jesus in the temple as an excuse to justify anger, repent before God and seek His help for future victory over anger.

2 Jesus Made a Scourge

Application of John 2:15

"When he [Jesus] had made a scourge [whip] of small cords, he drove them all out of the temple, and the sheep, and the oxen; and poured out the changers' money, and overthrew the tables" (John 2:15).

Think of a time that your anger seemed justified. In light of that incident and with careful consideration of the following two passages of Scripture, answer the questions below.

Read John 2:17 and Psalm 69:7–9.

1. In Psalm 69, David was sharing his heart with God. For whose sake did he suffer?_____

2. For whose sake did Jesus suffer shame, dishonor, and reproach?

   _____

3. Do you get angry because God has been offended or because you (or those with whom you identify) are offended?_____

   _____

4. Is your anger a result of zeal for God, or zeal for yourself? (zeal = *qinah* = jealousy, envy)[1] _____

5. How would zeal for God be exhibited differently than zeal for self?

   _____

   _____

Read John 2:15–19, Matthew 21:12–16, and Mark 11:15–19.

6. According to the verses you just read, describe the reaction of those who saw Jesus' action of "anger."

Disciples: _____

Crowd: _____

Children: _____

Jewish officials: _____

Was any of these responses a normal reaction to anger?

_____

7. How do people react to you when you are angry? _____

_____

8. Was Jesus reacting to what He saw in the temple, or was He obeying His Father? _____

_____

9. When you are angry, do you react or act according to God's guidance (under His authority)? Do you demonstrate the humility of one who is under authority? _____

10. Can you justify your anger by comparing it to Jesus' anger as He drove out the money changers? _____

Pray: Ask God to help you remain under His authority, being pro-active with others rather than reacting in anger. If you have justified your anger, ask God to forgive you.

Digging Deeper:

Jeremiah 11:19–20   1 Peter 5:5–7
John 5:30   Isaiah 53:6–7
Proverbs 15:33   2 Timothy 1:8–9

3 Warning Signs

"When they heard these things, they were cut to the heart, and they gnashed on him with their teeth" (Acts 7:54).

Read Acts 7:51–60 and Matthew 5:20–22.
    (For the whole story, read Acts 6:9–7:60.)

If there is even a little truth in an accusation or confrontation, we usually become angry—and we are probably angry more often than we realize. In order to overcome our anger, we need to recognize its signs. We can gain wisdom from the passage in Acts 7 as we observe the actions of those who were enraged at Stephen.

The first sign of the officials' anger was that they gnashed their teeth; then they cried out with a loud voice. If we would notice when we clench our teeth (tense our muscles), we might be able to catch ourselves before our voices become loud, tense, or harsh.

Next, the officials covered their ears! (v. 57) One sign of anger is no longer being open to hearing what the other person has to say. It becomes impossible to reason with an angry person. The intensity grows, and generally the volume increases as each tries to make himself heard.

Sometimes we become silent and shut down, but we still refuse to listen to the other person. Sullen silence is just as much an expression of anger as yelling is, and it can be just as damaging. Either way, we close our ears to others.

The angry crowd rushed on Stephen "with one accord" and ran him out of the city! (vv. 57–58) When we are angry with others, we may not run them out of the city, but we reject them and close our hearts to them. Like the city officials, we don't plan to do this. It's by impulse that our spirits close. In fact, we are unable to be angry with someone and at the same time have an open heart toward him/her.

The final expression of the crowd was to stone Stephen! (vv. 58–59) Once we indulge the full expression of our anger, it is very difficult to regain control. The anger seems to gain a life of its own, growing

Warning
Signs

stronger and louder. The angrier we get, the less rational we become, leading to actions we later regret.

While we don't generally go so far as to stone others to death, our anger is life-threatening to relationships. According to Jesus, it is likened to murder (Matt. 5:20–22).

Pray: Ask God to help you recognize the signs of anger and to be quick to refrain from anger, once you see the signs. Ask Him to show you the roots of your anger and to lead you to freedom.

3 Warning Signs
Application of Acts 7:54

"When they heard these things, they were cut to the heart, and they gnashed on him with their teeth" (Acts 7:54).

Learning to recognize the signs of anger and the types of things that trigger your anger can help you recognize the anger before it is expressed. As you recognize these signs, you can learn to conquer your angry responses rather than allowing them to conquer you.

1. Listed below are common expressions of anger. Check the ones that you have demonstrated. Underline the ones you demonstrate most often. (Ask for input from your family!)

  __ Clenched teeth   __ Not listening   __ Irritability

  __ Rapid breathing   __ Raised voice   __ Glaring

  __ Argumentation   __ Clenched fist   __ Swearing

  __ Silent treatment   __ Impatience   __ Hurtful words

  __ High-pitched voice __ Harsh, steely voice

  Other: _____

 Physical attack:

  __ On individuals   __ On surrounding objects

2. What usually makes you angry?

  __ Circumstances   __ Other people   __ Yourself

3. When do you get angry? (Check the ones that apply.)

  __ When afraid   __ When opposed

  __ When not heard   __ When jealous

  __ When losing face   __ When losing control

  __ When plans are thwarted

  __ When authority is questioned

  __ When facing unknown

  __ When expectation is not met

___ When hurt: ( ) emotionally ( ) physically

___ When a mistake is made: ( ) by others ( ) by yourself

___ Other

4. Anger is often a method of coping. Think about the reasons you get angry. What are you trying to accomplish when you get angry?

_____

_____

_____

5. Do you really want to conquer your anger? _____

6. What will you have to trust into God's hands to be an overcomer?

_____

_____

_____

7. Will you yield them to Him now?_____

Note: The next lesson is foundational for overcoming anger, and it has an extra section for application. Allow extra time and do not save your homework until the last minute in order to have time to complete the assignment.

Pray: Offer to God the things listed in #6.

Digging Deeper:

Genesis 4:3–9	Matthew 5:20–22
James 1:19–20	Psalm 37:1–9
Proverbs 14:29	Proverbs 16:32
Proverbs 19:11	Proverbs 25:28

4 You Choose

"Be ye angry, and sin not: let not the sun go down upon your wrath: neither give place to the devil" (Ephesians 4:26–27).

Read Psalm 4:1–8.

Is God commanding us to be angry? Many think this verse justifies anger. However, a closer look at the words gives clearer understanding. The verb for *be ye angry* is one word in the Greek, and it is written in the passive tense, having the sense of "when you are exasperated or angered." The passive tense implies that something is done that makes you angry. "When something happens that makes you angry, don't sin."

Paul is acknowledging the fact that we get angry, that it is a natural, human reaction. But he also warns us to not sin, to not let the sun go down on our wrath. It is inevitable; things will happen and we will become angry. However, Paul exhorts us to work through our passions and emotions over things that have been done to us—and to do so before the sun goes down.

As David was fleeing from Absalom, he wrote, "Stand in awe, and sin not" (Ps. 4:4). *Stand in awe* means to tremble or rage with violent emotion, especially from anger or fear! David was being wronged, and he was in danger. He had all the natural factors that lead to raging anger, and yet he wrote, ". . . and sin not." We know that for David the natural response was to be angry, because as he spoke to his own heart, he counseled himself to be still and quiet. He chose to not be angry.

When we are wronged, our natural response is anger, but that is indeed the natural response, the response of the flesh. God commands us to not sin when we are angered. Rather than justifying our temper or by taking things into our own hands, we have to choose to receive the grace of God to overcome the anger, and to trust God.

Pray: Ask God to forgive you for the times you have sinned as a result of anger. (Be specific if God brings specific situations to mind.) Ask God to teach you to deal with your sin of anger and to help you walk in righteousness.

4 You Choose

Application of Ephesians 4:26

"Be ye angry, and sin not: let not the sun go down upon your wrath: neither give place to the devil" (Ephesians 4:26–27).

I. The first step in overcoming anger is to admit that it is sin.

Read Galatians 5:19–21, Colossians 3:8, and Matthew 5:21–22.

1. According to these verses, what is God's view of anger?_____

_____

2. When you are angry, against whom do you sin? _____

3. If the other person is 95% wrong, does that mean you did not sin when you became angry? _____

    List by name the people with whom you are most often angry:

    _____

    _____

    _____

    List the most recent times that you were angry:_____

    _____

    _____

II. The second step in overcoming anger is to accept personal responsibility for your angry reactions.

Read Revelation 20:12.

4. What does God hold you accountable for? _____

You cannot make the other person repent, but you are held responsible for your own actions, and you can take steps to correct your relationship with God and with others.

Pray. Ask God to help you see what your responsibility was when you got angry. How was your heart not pure before Him? (Examples: pride, self-centeredness, greed, expectations)

Read Matthew 5:22–24.

(In verse 23, note the placement of the word *therefore*.)

5. If someone has something against you, how does it affect your relationship with him/her? _____

_____

_____

6. How does it affect your relationship with God?_____

_____

7. What does God instruct you to do about it? _____

_____

_____

8. Are you willing to obey God on this matter? (You will find peace only through obedience.) _____

9. List (by name) those to whom you have shown anger and have not cleared the offense._____

_____

_____

10. Follow the "Steps to Gain a Clear Conscience" (next page) on how to go and make things right with them.

Pray. Ask the Lord for the grace to take personal responsibility and to obey Him in gaining a clear conscience.

Digging Deeper:

Psalm 24:14   Philippians 2:1–4
Hebrews 12:14–15   1 Peter 3:10–12

Continue the application of these truths by completing Steps to Gain a Clear Conscience in the exercise below.

"But the goal of our instruction is love from a pure heart and a good conscience and a sincere faith" (1 Timothy 1:5, NASB).

Steps to Gain a Clear Conscience

I. Confess your sin to God and ask Him to forgive you for your anger.

Read 1 John 1:9.

    A. Ask the Lord to help you see where you were wrong.

    B. With God's help, identify the attitudes of your heart that did not represent God's attitudes in those situations.

    C. Pray, asking God's forgiveness where you were wrong.

II. Forgive the other person for what he did that prompted your anger.

Read Matthew 6:14–15.

    A. If the hurt is deep, making it difficult to forgive, read Matthew 18:21–35. (Put yourself in the story and ponder what God has done for you.)

    B. Pray, telling God you forgive that person.

Note: If you have forgiven the person with whom you were angry but the harsh, critical attitude remains (or continues to come back), you will need to deal with bitterness in order to find freedom. Steps for freedom from bitterness can be found with the "Be Not Bitter" meditation (Lesson 13).

III. Go to those whom you have offended with your anger and ask each one for forgiveness.

A. Prepare. Determine beforehand what you will say.

　✳ Keep it brief.
　✳ Do not place any blame on the other person.
　✳ Do not defend yourself or explain why you got angry.

Say something like this: *"The Lord has convicted me that I was wrong when I got angry. Would you forgive me?"*

Do not say, *"I'm sorry."* Ask for forgiveness. If the individual is not willing to respond positively, express your desire, but don't push. Give the Lord time to work in his heart.

It is even better to also ask forgiveness for your wrong attitudes.

Example: *"The Lord showed me that when I got angry at you, I was being prideful and not being considerate of you. Would you forgive me for my pride, my lack of consideration, my anger, and the hurt I caused you?"*

B. Ask the Lord to prepare the other person to receive you and to bring about reconciliation.

C. Seek the Lord concerning the best time to go to each person you have offended. Ask God to give you a pure heart and genuine love for them.

D. Go in obedience to God, using the wording you prepared ahead of time. Trust God for reconciliation, rather than trying to make the other person change.

5 Truth and Consequences

"A man of great wrath shall suffer punishment: for if thou deliver him, yet thou must do it again" (Proverbs 19:19).

Read Romans 2:4–10.

There are unavoidable consequences of anger. God tells us that an angry person will suffer punishment. If you rescue him from the punishment (consequences), you will have to rescue him again and again, because the angry person will continue to get angry. Anger does not go away when left alone.

In this one verse, three lessons stand out for the man of great wrath:

✳ There are consequences each time I become angry.

✳ If the anger remains hidden and covered and is not dealt with, it will continue to erupt, again and again.

✳ Expecting someone else to cover for me—shielding me from the consequences—is actually expecting him to help me remain an angry person and is thus making him a part of the problem.

We need to understand that even when anger seems justified, there are consequences for becoming angry. The punishment for my anger is sure, and those around me also will suffer the consequences. Rather than expecting those who are closest to me to deliver me and cover for me, I need to allow them to hold me accountable each time I am angry.

If I love those who are close to me, I will stop blaming them for my anger. It is my problem. It is my responsibility. In this verse, God is telling those around me to stop taking responsibility for my problem and stop covering for me.

If I love them, I will not hold them responsible. If I love God, I will no longer blame others but will fall on my face before Him, for He is my help and my salvation.

Truth and
Consequences

Pray: Ask God to forgive you for your anger, for trying to ignore and excuse it, and for blaming others rather than taking personal responsibility for it. Ask God to wash you and to create a clean heart within you. Commit to take personal responsibility for your sins and shortcomings, and ask for God's strength and courage to do so.

5 Truth and Consequences

Application of Proverbs 19:19

"A man of great wrath shall suffer punishment: for if thou deliver him, yet thou must do it again" (Proverbs 19:19).

1. List some consequences you have suffered because of someone else's anger. _____

   _____

2. List some consequences that those you love have suffered because of your anger. _____

   _____

3. List the names of those you have expected to deliver you from the consequences of your anger. _____

   _____

Pray: Ask God to forgive you for not taking responsibility for your actions. Release those around you from the blame and responsibility you have put on them.

Follow the guidelines on pages 21 and 23–24 for gaining a clear conscience. It is important to not try to defend or explain yourself in any way.

Read 1 John 1:5–9.

4. Can someone walk in fellowship with God while holding anger?

   _____

5. How can we be assured that we have fellowship with one another?

   _____

   _____

6. What do we need to do to be sure that we stay in fellowship? (v. 9)

_____

_____

_____

7. What does James 5:16 say concerning confessions?

_____

_____

_____

Accountability Partners: An accountability partner will help you walk in the light as you go to him and confess your sins every time you become angry. Pray for God to lead. It needs to be someone who is mature in the Lord and who will direct you back to the Lord and His forgiveness.

8. Whom do you know who would qualify as an accountability partner?

_____

9. Are you willing to humble yourself to another person in order to walk in the light and be healed?

_____

Pray: Ask God to show you whom you can go to for accountability. Commit to the Lord to take responsibility for your anger rather than blaming those around you.

Digging Deeper:

Galatians 6:7   Proverbs 19:11
1 John 1:7   John 3:19
Revelation 2:23

6 Seeking Destruction

*"He loveth transgression that loveth strife: and he that exalteth
his gate seeketh destruction"* (Proverbs 17:19).

Read Romans 13:1–7.

Transgression and strife go hand and hand. If we find ourselves frequently in the midst of strife, it is a sign that we love transgression! Transgression in this verse involves more than wrongdoing. The idea of revolt, or breaking away from authority, is included in the definition. We may protest that we don't revolt and that we only stretch the boundaries and do our own thing. However, the issue is whether or not we remain under the authority that God placed over us.

The second part of Proverbs 17:19 emphasizes the same point. The meaning for *exalteth* is "to be proud." At the time the book of Proverbs was written, it was common for the city leaders to meet at the gate of the city. Therefore, if we are exalting our gate, we are exalting ourselves above the leaders who sit in authority over us. We are being our own boss.

To paraphrase the verse, if we love being our own boss, we love strife. God established authority structures. Whether in the family, in government, in churches, or in business, if we follow God's plan for us to honor authorities, we experience protection and peace. If we choose instead to follow our own counsel and desires, we will surely come to strife.

God established authority, and He placed each of us under authority. Therefore, when we choose to follow our own agenda, it is really God whom we are resisting. We are putting ourselves above God and declaring that we know how to run our lives better than He does! If we choose to resist God, can we really expect peace in our lives?

Pray: Confess the sin of loving your own way and resisting authority, and ask God to forgive you. Commit to obey God by honoring and obeying the authorities He placed over you.

6 Seeking Destruction

Application of Proverbs 17:19

"He loveth transgression that loveth strife: and he that exalteth his gate seeketh destruction" (Proverbs 17:19).

1. List the names of the authority figures in your life.
   (Note: According to Scripture, at the time of marriage the husband and wife are released from the governing authority of parents. Upon marriage, the man becomes the authority in his home. The wife is to submit to her husband, but she would also be in authority over the children. At that point they look to their parents for counsel.)

   Family _____

   Church _____

   Work _____

   Government _____

2. In which of the four areas listed above do you "love transgression"?

   _____

   More specifically, whom do you resist who is in authority over you?

   _____

3. In what circumstances do you decide what you will do instead of following your authority? _____

   _____

4. **Read** and paraphrase Romans 13:1–2. _____

   _____

   _____

   _____

Pray: Repent of your rebellion and willfulness (stubbornly doing as you please).

Make a commitment to trust God to work through your authorities.

Note: It may seem that the person who is in authority over you is not worthy of your submission. However, the path of obedience to God, and thus to peace, is submission. Of course, if your authority asks you to do something that is opposed to the principles established by God, you should choose to obey God, even if that means disobeying your authority. We can appeal and sometimes bring change, but appeals also need to be made in the spirit of submission. On the other hand, never disobey God in an attempt to submit to authority.

Digging Deeper:

Family:	Matthew 19:5	Ephesians 6:2–3
	Ephesians 5:22–24, 33	
Church:	1 Timothy 5:17	1 Peter 5:1–5
	Titus 1:5	
Work:	Titus 2:9–10	
Government:	Titus 3:1	Hebrews 13:17

7 Let Go and Let God

"Cease from anger, and forsake wrath: fret not thyself in any wise to do evil" (Psalm 37:8).

Read Psalm 37:1–11.

Sometimes we enjoy being angry. We reject the thought to cease from anger, choosing instead to express the negative emotions that seethe within. To do so is to disobey God. The word *cease* (*rapha*) means "to slacken, to let it alone, or to let go." God tells us to slacken our hold on our anger. We are to turn loose, to let it go, to drop it.

In this one verse, we are told not only to cease from anger, but we are also told to forsake wrath. *Forsake* (*azab*) means "to fail, to relinquish, to leave." Rather than hold on to anger, as we are tempted to do, God clearly commands us to relinquish our hold on it and leave it behind us.

The verse continues, telling us not to fret (*charah*, "to burn with anger"), because it will only lead to evil. Three times in one verse, using three different words, God admonishes us not to be angry, adding that anger leads to evil.

God is not trying to make life difficult by asking us to strangle our emotions. He is a loving Father, seeking to protect us from the evil that is unavoidable if we hold on to our anger.

At the moment I am tempted to be angry, the choice is mine. Will I hold onto my emotions and my efforts to take care of things my way? Or will I let go and let God be God, trusting Him to work out things—even if He handles them differently than I would?

I cannot hold onto the anger and trust God at the same time. If I want to walk in victory, I must learn to obey the first prompting of the Holy Spirit to accept His grace and to "let go." If I am not immediately obedient, and choose instead to express the anger I am feeling, I reject the Lord's grace. As I reject Him, I side against God, and the battle is even more difficult to turn around.

**Let Go and
Let God**

Pray: Ask God to enable you to trust Him when you are feeling angry and to give you the courage to "let go" and "let God" be God, trusting yourself and your interests into His care.

7 Let Go and Let God

Application of Psalm 37:8

"Cease from anger, and forsake wrath: fret not thyself in any wise to do evil" (Psalm 37:8).

1. In the moment of anger, why do you want to hang onto your anger?

   _____

   _____

   _____

   _____

2. Which is really more important—winning for the moment, or obeying God? _____

If obeying God and walking in His ways are more important, talk to Him about it:

   ❋ Confess your sin of choosing to be angry, and ask God to forgive you.

   ❋ Ask Him to wash you with His blood, cleansing you from the unrighteousness of anger.

   ❋ Ask Him to teach you and give you grace (the desire and the strength) to walk in His ways.

3. **Read** the following verses, noting that in the book of Psalms the verses use the words *rapha* and *azab* in relation to us, and in Deuteronomy 31 the same words are used while speaking of God.

   ❋ Psalm 37:8: "Cease (*rapha*) from anger, and forsake (*azab*) wrath . . . ."

   ❋ Psalm 46:10: "Be still (*rapha*), and know that I am God."

   ❋ Deuteronomy 31:6: "Be strong and of a good courage, fear not, nor be afraid of them: for the Lord thy God, he it is that doth go with thee; he will not fail (*rapha*) thee, nor forsake (*azab*) thee."

rapha = cease, slack, let go, let it alone

azab = fail, relinquish, leave[2]

4. What do you need to "let go"? Why do you need to "let go" in order to "be still"? _____

_____ .

_____

How does knowing that He is God affect your ability to "let go"?

_____

_____

How important is it that you know that He is God, in order for you to be still? _____

_____

5. If you be still (let go) and know that He is God, how does it affect your anger? _____

_____

6. What difference does it make to know that He will not fail me or forsake me? _____

_____

_____

6b. How can I apply that truth in the moment when I am tempted to be angry? _____

_____

It is impossible to hold onto anger and to God at the same time. You must choose.

Digging Deeper:

Deuteronomy 30:19–20   Deuteronomy 32:4
Deuteronomy 7:9   2 Thessalonians 3:3
Psalm 9:10   Psalm 37:3–5

8 Put It Off!

"But now ye also put off all these; anger, wrath, malice, blasphemy, filthy communication out of your mouth" (Colossians 3:8).

Read Colossians 1:9–14.

We tend to justify an eruption of anger by blaming others or blaming the circumstances. We also feel that if we suppress our anger and don't express it through violence or outbursts that it causes no harm. We further reason that it is therefore not a problem.

However, God says to put off the anger that we have been justifying. He calls it evil (Ps. 37:8) and says that if we are angry with a brother without a cause, we are guilty of murder (Matt. 5:22).

We cannot conquer our anger without first dealing with our hearts. God's direction to us is to put off all anger and wrath (from the heart), along with their accompanying outward expressions: malice, blasphemy, and vile talk.

God speaks repeatedly against anger because He knows our shortcomings, and He knows that we need to be told the seriousness of our sin. However, most people who try to put off their anger fail in their attempts. If we focus on the anger in our attempts to overcome that anger, we will strive in futility.

In order to gain victory, our focus needs to be on God, not on our anger nor on ourselves. We also need to realize that we can't conquer anger by ourselves. We need God's grace and power in order to overcome it.

In spite of our failures, there is hope. God would not tell us to put off anger if we were destined to always be angry. We can be changed as we yield to the Holy Spirit living within us. He will not force Himself on us; we must surrender to Him.

Like John the Baptist, we must come to the point of saying, "He must increase, but I must decrease" (John 3:30). As we take up our cross daily

Put It Off!

and say, "Not my will, but thine be done," we will be available for God to work within us, and we can overcome damaging patterns of anger.

As we seek to obey God's command to put off anger, we have two choices: (1) continue to struggle to put off our anger—and experience growing frustration, or (2) die to our own selfish will and our own strength—and let God work within us.

Pray. Confess choosing your own way and walking in your own strength. Express your desire to be surrendered to Him. Ask Him to teach you how to surrender. Pray that He might increase and you might decrease.

8 Put It Off!

Application of Psalm 37:8

"But now ye also put off all these; anger, wrath, malice, blasphemy, filthy communication out of your mouth" (Colossians 3:8).

Without God's help, we cannot successfully put off our anger. We must depend on the Lord to do it within us. In order to experience victory over anger, we need to surrender to Him control of the areas from which our anger grows.

1. Underline the areas listed below in which you need for God to take control in your life.

   Fears   Opposition   Authority   Plans

   Control   Expectations   Hurts   Perfection

   Rights: to be heard, to have my way, to be loved, to be respected, to be informed, to be cared for, _____.

   Other: _____

2. Copy down each area underlined in the question above. Beside each one, name some specific battles that you face regularly. (Examples: Fears—of not being good enough, of my spouse leaving me, of failure, etc.; Authority—struggle against my parents, and bosses, etc.)

   _____

   _____

   _____

   _____

   _____

   _____

   _____

   _____

   _____

   _____

Put It Off!

Pray:

* Yield your life to God in each of the applicable areas above.

* Give Jesus the things that make you angry, trusting them into His care.

* Confess the sin of not trusting Him with each area of your life. (Picture yourself placing each one on the altar at His feet when you pray. It is now His, and you have no more right to it.)

* Ask Him to show you when you try to pick it back up off the altar, and to give you the grace to leave it with Him when you are tempted to pick it back up.

Digging Deeper:

Anger is sin: Psalm 37:8, Matthew 5:22

Reasons to not be angry: Ephesians 2:10, 1 Corinthians 3:16, 2 Corinthians 3:3, James 1:20

Path to victory: John 3:30, Luke 22:42, Luke 9:23

Hope for victory over anger: Philippians 3:14, Psalm 31:24, Psalm 39:7–9

9 Vain Religion

"If any man among you seem to be religious, and bridleth not his tongue, but deceiveth his own heart, this man's religion is vain" (James 1:26).

Read James 1:19–26 and 1 Peter 3:10–13.

Many of us are admired for our dedication to God and the seemingly selfless way in which we serve. However, our tongues are sometimes used as tools of destruction when only family members are near. God says that if our tongues are not under His Lordship (i.e., His control), we are deceived, and our religion is in vain—even if we are church leaders.

James 1:19–26 speaks of the need to control the tongue in the spreading of gossip and in filthy talk, but the focus is mostly on anger, especially in verses 19 and 26. If we don't control our tongues, we deceive ourselves and our religion is in vain. It is useless.

How could religion be useless? God is certainly not purposeless, nor is His Word unavailing! What could make religion useless? If we have an infection and go to the doctor for healing, it is in vain that we go if we decide not to take the prescription given by the doctor to fight the infection. Likewise, when we go to church and read our Bibles expecting help but do not apply the Word to our lives, is it not useless? Our religion becomes vain when we don't apply God's truths to our lives.

In order to determine if this passage applies to me, I must ask myself, "Do I bridle my tongue?" If the answer is no, then I need to discover where I am deceived and how my religion is useless. The problem is not with religion—at least not with God. The problem is that I have failed to apply God's Word and allow Him to do the needed work in my life.

Pray. Ask the Lord's forgiveness for not applying His truths in your life. Yield yourself to Him for His work to be done, particularly in the area of controlling your tongue and overcoming anger.

9 Vain Religion
Application of James 1:26

"If any man among you seem to be religious, and bridleth not his tongue, but deceiveth his own heart, this man's religion is vain" (James 1:26).

Read John 8:32–37.

1. What would keep the truth from setting you free? (v. 37) _____

   _____

2. If you are not free (if you still struggle with anger and an unbridled tongue), whom are you serving? _____

   _____

Read 2 Timothy 3:5, 7.

3. Is God's power in your life? If yes, do you draw from it when angry?

   _____

   _____

4. If your answer to either question is no, how are you denying the power of God in your life? _____

   _____

   _____

5. As you are learning of God, what is blocking the knowledge of Him in your life? _____

   _____

   _____

Read James 3:1–18.

6. What is the problem with the tongue? _____

_____

7. Why do we have such a problem with the tongue? (vv. 14–18)

_____

_____

Read Matthew 12:34–35.

8. Why does Jesus say that the tongue has such a problem? _____

_____

_____

Read Psalm 51:5–6.

9. How were you conceived and how were you shaped? _____

_____

You can do nothing to cleanse or change your heart. Just as you cannot save yourself, you cannot cleanse yourself. The good news is that God can do these things for you, and He is waiting to be asked!

Read Psalm 51:7–17.

Pray. Personalize this passage as a prayer to God for the cleansing and renewal of your heart. Use it as a guide for your prayer, but express your heart to the Lord as He guides you by His Holy Spirit.

Vain
Religion

Digging Deeper:

Proverbs 12:18	Romans 1:18
1 Peter 3:9–10	John 17:17–19
Psalm 15:1–3	Psalm 34:12–14
Proverbs 18:21	Proverbs 21:23
Isaiah 64:6	Psalm 25:3–5
1 Corinthians 6:11	Revelation 1:5–6

10 Surrendered Love

"But now abide faith, hope, love, these three; but the greatest of these is love" (1 Corinthians 13:13, NASB).

Read Mark 12:29–31 and 1 John 4:7–21.

In a word, the cure for anger is love. "The greatest of these is love" has become so familiar that we no longer really listen to those words when they are spoken, but the truth remains: the greatest of these is love. God isn't talking about the self-centered "feel-good" that is sought by the world today. True love is the self-sacrificing love that Jesus demonstrated.

We would not have a problem with anger if we could learn to love our God with all our hearts. If loving with all our hearts is too difficult, we are given terms that are not quite so demanding: we can love our neighbor as ourselves! There is only one problem: we're not able to do that without first knowing the love of the Father. The second command is dependent on the first.

Jesus' love was "other-centered." Because of His love for us, He yielded the things that we grasp for in our anger. He surrendered His rights, reputation, power, acceptance, and control. He sacrificed them so that we could be saved and could then fellowship with Him.

That kind of love is beyond us. In fact, we can no more love with such sacrificial love than we can save ourselves. To truly love others, we are totally dependent on God, just as we are dependent on Him for our salvation. We must surrender our hearts to Him and allow Him to love others through us.

This process begins with us asking. We are told to ask—and we will receive, to seek—and we will find, but we will not always receive and find instantaneously (Matt. 7:7–11). As you continue to surrender yourselves to God, asking Him to love others through you, one day you will realize that you have spontaneously and genuinely expressed love in a way that is beyond you. As you continue to seek Him and to walk in His righteousness, He will transform your heart into a heart that loves.

Surrendered Love

Pray: Ask God to forgive you for trying to love others in your own strength. Surrender your heart to Him. Ask Him to fill your heart with love for Him and to love others through you.

10 Surrendered Love

Application of I Corinthians 13:13

"But now abide faith, hope, love, these three; but the greatest of these is love" (1 Corinthians 13:13, NASB).

Read Matthew 12:34.

1. Love is internal; it is hidden in the heart. However, according to this verse, what external sign will there be as to whether or not we have love in our hearts?_____

2. If we think we love, and say we love, but speak evil, what does that say about our hearts?_____

Read 1 Corinthians 13:1–8a.

3. In verses 1–3, what things that we admire and value as being spiritual are mentioned? _____

4. What does God say about them? _____

5. What does 1 Corinthians 13:13 indicate? _____

_____

Love is important to God. In this chapter we are told what love is like, so we have a standard of how we are to act toward others. In order to find what is hidden in our hearts, we need to think of how the mouth speaks when we are not exercising self-control, i.e., when we are angry, because it is out of the abundance of the heart that the mouth speaks.

In the list below, check off the items that describe your behavior when the hidden heart is showing. Examine your heart to see where you fall short of reflecting the glory of God.

Love:

v. 4 _____ Suffers long _____ Is kind
_____ Is not jealous/does not envy
_____ Is not rash/does not brag
_____ Is not proud/arrogant

v. 5 _____ Does not act unbecomingly
_____ Does not seek its own
_____ Is not easily provoked
_____ Does not take account of a wrong suffered

v. 6 _____ Does not rejoice in unrighteousness
_____ Rejoices in the truth

v. 7 _____ Bears all things
_____ Believes all things
_____ Hopes all things
_____ Endures all things

v. 8 _____ Never fails

"So shall My word be which goes forth from My mouth; It shall not return to Me empty, Without accomplishing what I desire, And without succeeding in the matter for which I sent it"
(Isa. 55:11, NASB).

3. Pray: Ask God to forgive you for your lack of love.

4. Write these verses (1 Corinthians 13:4–8a) on another piece of paper, spaced to emphasize each point.

   ❋ Keep it in your Bible to use regularly as a reminder and guide for prayer.

   ❋ When angered, use these verses as a standard to bring repentance and to grow.

   ❋ When tension is building in a relationship, read over this chapter, allowing God to point out the area you need to work on. Do it before you explode.

   ❋ Repent of the unrighteousness in your heart before it is expressed in actions.

5. Pray. Ask God to fill your heart with His love for others. You cannot make yourself love another person, and God wants you to grow in love. His strength will be made known in your weakness as you cry out to Him.

Digging Deeper:

1 Timothy 1:5

John 13:35

John 15:4–5, 9, 11

Ezekiel 36:26

Matthew 22:36 40

Philippians 2:13

Proverbs 10:12

1 John 4:7–8, 16

2 Corinthians 12:9–10

11 Be Ye Kind

"Let all bitterness, and wrath, and anger, and clamor, and evil speaking, be put away from you, with all malice: And be ye kind one to another, tenderhearted, forgiving one another, even as God for Christ's sake hath forgiven you" (Ephesians 4:31–32).

Read 1 Peter 3:8–19.

If we were not told that things such as bitterness, wrath, and clamor are unacceptable, we would justify them and hang on to them. However, after we see that they are not of God and attempt to conquer them, we are often frustrated.

One reason we have difficulty is that we focus on the thing we are trying to overcome. This wrong focus is counter-productive and leads to defeat. The most effective way to put unacceptable behavior behind us is to work on positive behavior, such as being kind, tenderhearted, and forgiving.

As we seek to be kind and tenderhearted, we need to think of others rather than to think of ourselves. To do so requires that we put ourselves in their position, thinking about how they feel and what they need. As we become sensitive to their needs and learn to lay down our own desires in order to meet their needs, we will grow in Christlike character. We will then struggle less and less with bitterness, wrath, anger, clamor, and evil speaking.

We are also told to forgive "one another, even as God, for Christ's sake hath forgiven" us. Actually, we cannot consistently be genuinely kind and tenderhearted toward someone we have not forgiven. Genuine forgiveness is foundational to being kind and tenderhearted.

When God forgave us, He did not draw boundaries, declaring that some things hurt too much or were too bad to forgive. He took all our sin, taking the penalty of our sin upon Himself. We could not have paid the price ourselves.

Be Ye
Kind

Steps for forgiving are
given in the Application Page.

In our relationships, we need to follow the example of Jesus, being kind and tenderhearted, forgiving others in the same way we have been forgiven. We need to be quick to forgive, forgive when it hurts, and be willing to forgive frequently. Only by forgiving can we be freed from the bondage to unacceptable behaviors—the bondage of anger.

Pray: Ask God to show you any unforgiveness in your heart, and ask Him to forgive you. Forgive all those whom you have not forgiven and release them into God's hands.

11 Be Ye Kind

Application of Ephesians 4:31-32

"Let all bitterness, and wrath, and anger, and clamor, and evil speaking, be put away from you, with all malice: And be ye kind one to another, tenderhearted, forgiving one another, even as God for Christ's sake hath forgiven you" (Ephesians 4:31–32).

Read Matthew 6:14–15.

1. What happens if we forgive others when they have wronged us?

_____

_____

_____

2. What happens if we do not forgive them? _____

_____

_____

Read Matthew 18:21–35.

3. In this parable, whom does the King (Lord) represent? _____

4. Which character represents us? _____

5. Has the King forgiven us? _____

_____

6. What does the King require of us? _____

_____

Anger is a tormentor
that comes from
unforgiveness;
it will continue to
torment us as long
as we have
unforgiveness.

7. What are the consequences for us if we do not forgive others?

_____

8. What qualifying phrase does Jesus use to describe forgiveness?

_____

_____

9. What are some tormentors of body, soul, and spirit that result from unforgiveness? _____

_____

_____

Read Galatians 6:7–8.

10. When you forgive someone, does it erase the consequences of their actions? _____

_____

_____

Forgiving someone is a legal transaction in which you release the offender into God's hands; it is not determined by how you feel about the offender, nor does it release him from consequences he might suffer as a result of his sin. As you forgive, confess your sin in the matter and ask God to change your heart so it will be pleasing to Him.

Sample prayer of forgiving: *Heavenly Father, even as you have forgiven me, I forgive (name) for (offense) and for the pain (be specific) it caused me. I release him/her into your hands, and I ask you to forgive me for (your sin). Please wash me in the blood of Christ and make my attitudes and feelings toward (name) pleasing to You.*

11. Pray through the prayer above, forgiving all those who have offended you. Be specific about how you were wronged, about how

it hurt, and about your sin. Ask God to show you whom you need to forgive. Tomorrow, or next month, when someone else comes to mind, pray through the prayer again so you can maintain a clear conscience and be free from tormentors.

Digging Deeper:

Matthew 6:12–15

Matthew 18:15–17

Psalm 24:3–4

Luke 6:27–38

Colossians 3:12–14

Matthew 5:38–40

Matthew 5:8–9

Matthew 7:1–5

2 Peter 1:4–11

12 Whose Standard?

*"But unto Cain, and to his offering he [God] had not respect. And
Cain was very wroth, and his countenance fell"* (Genesis 4:5).

Read Genesis 4:1–15.

This first mention of anger in the Bible gives us insight into a basic
root of all anger. Because God did not accept Cain's offering, Cain was
irate. He thought the offering that he gave was acceptable, even pleasing, and he expected God to be pleased. He wasn't willing to accept
God's standard for his offering.

We often fall into the trap of giving our best to God rather than seeking Him for what He would have us bring to Him. Our offering could
be expressed in gifts, in offerings, in time, in service, or even in worship. If we are pleased, we expect God to be pleased. When what we
offer to God isn't accepted, it shows that our standards aren't acceptable to God, and we respond in anger.

We tend to expect others to want the things we want and to be pleased
with the things that please us. Anger (whether toward God or toward
others) springs from that self-centeredness. In order to conquer anger,
we need to confess and repent of our self-centeredness and surrender
it to God.

For most of us, the central issue in anger is a focus on self and efforts
to gratify self rather than having God first in our lives. This love of self
could be expressed in pride, in greed, in unforgiveness, in expectations,
or in a desire to control. Each of these manifestations of self-love is a
root from which anger grows, and each comes from putting self above
God and those around us.

If our lives were Christ-centered, rather than self-centered, anger
wouldn't be a major problem in our lives, because we wouldn't be trying
to protect our standard or defend our offering. As we exchange our
standard for Christ's standard and yield our lives to Him, He will transform us from within. It is only through Christ and His love that we can

Whose Standard?

conquer self-centeredness—and the anger that results when God or others are not pleased with our offering.

Pray. Repent and ask God to forgive you for self-centeredness and for expecting God and others to meet your standards rather than seeking Him for His standards. Ask forgiveness for the anger that springs from self-centeredness.

12 Whose Standard?

Application of Genesis 4:5

"But unto Cain, and to his offering he [God] had not respect. And Cain was very wroth, and his countenance fell" (Genesis 4:5).

Read Genesis 4:3–8.

1. What did God say would happen to Cain's attitude if he responded correctly to God's correction? (v. 7) _____

_____

Note: A "fallen countenance" reveals anger in our hearts.

2. What if Cain does not respond righteously to God's correction? (v. 7)

_____

_____

3. Think of a time that you were not open to correction.

_____

_____

 ✳ How was your countenance, your attitude toward life, toward those around you, and toward God? _____

_____

_____

 ✳ Did you experience the consequence of further sin in your life? _____

_____

 ✳ How did you master the sin that was "crouching at your door"? If you didn't master it, what could you have done differently? _____

_____

_____

_____

Whose Standard?

"My food is to do the will of Him who sent me, and to accomplish His work" (John 4:34).

When our food (our sustenance, what keeps us going in life) is to accomplish God's work (meeting His standards, in obedience to Him), we will be in harmony with Him and will not struggle with anger.

If you are seeking to accomplish the Lord's work and find yourself continuing to struggle with anger or a fallen countenance, ask God to search your motives:

❋ Am I serving God and others as a form of worship to God, or is it out of duty? _____

❋ Am I truly surrendered to Him and His way, or am I seeking my own way? _____

❋ Am I serving so that He will receive the glory, or am I hoping for glory?_____

❋ Am I open to correction when God seeks to adjust me?

_____

Pray: Surrender to God the areas of your life that you have held onto.

Digging Deeper:

Matthew 6:33	Matthew 10:38–39
Matthew 16:24–26	1 Samuel 15:22
Proverbs 9:8	Proverbs 13:1
Revelation 3:19	Proverbs 3:11–12
Jeremiah 5:2–4	Proverbs 29:1
1 Peter 2:21	Romans 11:1–5

13 Be Not Bitter

"Husbands, love your wives, and be not bitter against them"
(Colossians 3:19).

Read James 3:9–16.

Why is this verse directed toward husbands? Could it be because men are less aware of their bitterness, rather than that men are more often bitter? This admonition to love your wives and not be bitter is written to husbands, but it follows an admonition to the wives to submit to their husbands as is fit in the Lord. Obviously, it is not fit for wives to be bitter against their husbands. Therefore, even though the husbands are specifically addressed, we all need to take heed.

Unrepentant anger breeds bitterness, but often we are not aware that we're bitter. Bitterness is manifested in a negative, critical, or judgmental attitude, which is often expressed in an angry, biting tone of voice. To determine if we are bitter, we can ask, "Am I constantly seeing fault with what my spouse—or someone else—does? Or says? Do I frequently correct and show displeasure rather than showing care and offering encouragement?" If that is the case, it is a sign that I am bitter.

A bitter, critical spirit destroys rather than builds. No one enjoys living with criticism. It makes little sense to tear down what we are working hard to build, but that's what we do when we harbor bitterness in a relationship.

Even when we are careful not to speak the criticism that lies within, a spouse can feel the bitter attitude. As a spouse experiences the negative, judgmental attitude, he/she becomes discouraged and begins to look outside the relationship for approval and possibly even for companionship.

Just as a bitter taste overwhelms positive flavors on the tongue, bitterness in our hearts taints entire relationships. The giving or receiving of a simple suggestion is felt as criticism or an attempt to control.

Be Not
Bitter

Bitterness erodes bonds of fellowship, leading to insensitivity, harshness, and angry displays with loved ones. It then overflows to harm relationships with many others. If we want to enjoy sweet fellowship, we need to get rid of bitterness.

Pray: Ask God to reveal any critical, judgmental attitude you are harboring. Confess it as sin and ask God to cleanse your heart. Ask Him to teach you to love, free from all bitterness, judgment, and criticism.

13 Be Not Bitter

Application of Colossians 3:19

"Husbands, love your wives, and be not bitter against them"
(Colossians 3:19).

"Be ye angry, and sin not: let not the sun go down upon your wrath: neither give place to the devil" (Eph. 4:26–27). Bitterness grows in our hearts as we go to bed angry, thereby giving ground in our souls to the devil. From that territory in the soul, Satan can attack, causing anger and other emotions such as anxiety, fear, and lust.

place = *topos*, a spot, or space of territory, ground[3]

Read Acts 8:18–23.

1. What did Peter see in Simon? (v. 23) _____
   (Others often see that we are bitter when we are not aware of it.)

2. As a result of his bitterness and iniquity, what consequences did Simon suffer? (vv. 20–21) _____

3. What was Peter's admonition to Simon? _____

   _____

4. What consequences have you experienced as a result of harboring bitterness? (vv. 20–21) _____

   _____

   _____

From insights gained in the following verses, list actions that will help you avoid future temptations to develop bitterness.

5. Luke 6:37 _____

   _____

Be Not Bitter

6. Ephesians 4:31–32 _____
_____

7. Philippians 4:8 _____
_____

8. 1 Thessalonians 5:16–18 _____
_____

Pray through the verses above, asking God to help you.

9. List the people toward whom you tend to feel judgmental and critical.
_____

10. List the people with whom you have been angry for several days.
_____

11. List the times you recall that you have held anger or bitterness toward your spouse. _____
_____

Use the answers in #9 through #11 as you work through "Overcoming Bitterness" on the following pages.

Digging Deeper:

Matthew 6:14–15
Psalm 50:6
Hebrews 12:14–15
James 3:10–18

Matthew 18:21–35
Psalm 51:5–10
Ephesians 4:31
Hebrews 12:23

Note: Continue to the next page to learn how to regain the ground you have given to the enemy through bitterness and how to restore your relationship with the people listed above.

©2007 Kay Camenisch • www.kaycamenisch.com

Overcoming Bitterness by Regaining Surrendered Ground

"Be ye angry, and sin not: let not the sun go down upon your wrath: neither give place to the devil" (Ephesians 4:26–27).

When you go to bed unrepentant of sin, you give "place" to the devil. *Place* is the root word from which we get the word *topography*. Every time we go to bed angry, we give the enemy title to some topography, territory, or ground—a place in our soul. From this ground that is now rightfully his, Satan can attack us and make us more easily angered (or despairing, fearful, lustful, prideful, depressed, etc.). Our sin gives him ground from which to attack. When we don't repent, we are giving the enemy legal permission to attack us.

Jesus Christ has won the victory for us so we can be free. However, since we give the ground to Satan by going to bed angry, we must ask God to regain that ground before we can experience the victory personally. Below are steps to take in order to regain the ground we have given away.

As you pray, be specific. Instead of praying "forgive me for my anger," ask God to forgive you for cursing your supervisor, yelling at a family member, or whatever action it was. Then confess the attitude behind the action, such as pride, self-centeredness, greed, impatience, etc.

1. Repent and confess your sins that led to the anger.

If you want to experience the righteousness, peace, and joy of kingdom living, repentance is the beginning point. Trace a particular time of anger back to the root sins that caused the anger, such as pride, holding rights, expectations, jealousy, guilt, etc. Be as specific and thorough as you can be with the sinful attitudes as well as the actions (Matt. 4:17). Then ask God to forgive you for the action and the attitude that was not pleasing to Him.

Be Not
Bitter

Note: Do not write your answers on this page so that you can use it over and over as a prayer guide when the Holy Spirit brings to your mind specific instances when you sinned against God and did not repent and ask for forgiveness before you went to bed.

"Repent: for the kingdom of heaven is at hand." "If we confess our sins, he is faithful and just to forgive us our sins, and to cleanse us from all unrighteousness" (Matt. 4:17b, 1 John 1:9).

"Father, I was wrong. Would you forgive me for ____(action)____. I sinned by ____(attitude or denial of God)_____."

2. Forgive the other person for any wrong that you feel was committed against you.

"For if you forgive men for their transgressions, your heavenly Father will also forgive you. But if you do not forgive men, then your Father will not forgive your transgressions" (Matt. 6:14–15, NASB).

"Father, I forgive ____(name)____ for ____(action)____, and for the _____(hurt, misunderstanding, frustration, anger . . .)_____ it caused me. I release him/her from all judgment on my part and trust him/her into Your hands."

3. Ask God to forgive you and wash you with His blood.

We are deserving of death for breaking God's commandments. If Jesus had not shed His precious blood for the cleansing of our sins, all of us would be condemned to eternal separation from God. Through Jesus' death, however, the debt we owed because of our sin is paid in full. As God's child, you can be washed clean from the sins mentioned above.

"In whom we have redemption through his blood, the forgiveness of sins, according to the riches of his grace" (Eph. 1:7).

"Father, wash me with Your blood and cleanse me from my sin(s) of _____."

4. Ask God to take back the ground that you surrendered.

"Neither give place to the devil" (Eph. 4:27).

"I ask you, Lord, to take back the ground that I gave to Satan when I _____(be specific about sinful actions and attitudes)_____."

Note: Be thorough. For each sin God brings to mind, repeat the process.

Your sins were specific; don't generalize your prayers for cleansing. Pray through these steps with each and every incident that God brings to mind.

(If the bitterness is deep, you may also need to forgive the person daily for an extended time before you experience freedom from bitterness.)

"And from the days of John the Baptist until now the kingdom of heaven suffereth violence, and the violent take it by force" (Matt. 11:12).

Be violent (thorough) in dealing with all sin that God brings to mind so you can experience the full freedom available to you.

5. Renew your mind with truth.

Satan is a liar. When he has territory in your soul, he attacks by whispering lies that seem like the truth. After regaining the ground, search the Scriptures for the truth to replace the lies that you have believed. Ask God to show you His truth. Memorize and meditate on His Word to renew your mind and soul.

"Do not be conformed to this world, but be transformed by the renewing of your mind, that you may prove what the will of God is, that which is good and acceptable and perfect" (Rom. 12:2, NASB).

Note: Ground can also be given to the enemy through other sins (see Ephesians 4 and 5). These same steps can be followed to gain victory over those sins as well. Some of the most dramatic deliverance and freedom we have seen have come as a result of asking God to reclaim ground that was given to the enemy through sins of willful disobedience and rebellion.

("Steps for Overcoming Bitterness by Regaining Surrendered Ground" is used by permission of the Institute in Basic Life Principles, Oak Brook, IL.)

14 Enslaved by Guilt

"Now therefore be not grieved, nor angry with yourselves, that ye sold me hither" (Genesis 45:5a).

Read Genesis 37:1–36.

After selling Joseph, as his brothers returned home they probably felt quite pleased with how smart they had been in disposing of their proud little brother. However, their father's grief was a constant reminder of their sin. They lived for years with guilt weighing on their shoulders.

Hidden sin and guilt breed anger. The first step in overcoming such anger is to acknowledge hidden sin.

While in captivity, the Lord moved Joseph to the position of a ruler in Egypt. Meanwhile a famine threatened the people of Israel with starvation, and Joseph's brothers went to Egypt to seek help. The official who was in charge of food distribution was Joseph. Joseph's brothers had to appeal to the very person whom they had sold into slavery. When Joseph revealed his identity to his brothers, he immediately brought their sin into the light, telling them not to be grieved and angry with themselves for what they had done to him.

When we are ashamed of our actions, we tend to hide them, wishing we could forget about them. We don't feel deserving of God's forgiveness, and we become angry with ourselves. As a result, pressure builds, making us ready to explode at any time. If we want to release the pent-up anger, we need to confess so God can release us from our sin and wash the guilt away.

Until it's forgiven, sin hinders relationships with God and with others. For years Joseph had been like a man without a family. He didn't want merely to know about his family; he wanted to *be* family, to enjoy fellowship with them. But first there needed to be restoration from past sins.

After revealing his identity, Joseph immediately sought to clear past wrongs so he and his brothers could enjoy fellowship with one another.

Enslaved by
Guilt

Note: For Steps to Forgiveness, see Lesson 4, "You Choose."

Just as God wants a deep, personal relationship with us, Joseph wanted intimacy with his brothers, not just to know how they were doing.

Few of us have sold a family member into slavery, but many of us are enslaved by guilt—and by the anger and bitterness that grow out of it. God wants to free us and to enjoy fellowship with us, but first we need to come to Him and repent of any hidden sin.

Pray. Ask God to search your heart and show you if there is any hidden sin you have not confessed to Him. (Give the Lord time to respond! It will probably take time. Keep your ear open to Him for days after you ask.) Repent of any hidden sin, asking God to forgive you. Forgive yourself. Go to those you have offended and ask their forgiveness. Make any restitution if that is appropriate.

14 Enslaved by Guilt

Application of Colossians 3:19

"Now therefore be not grieved, nor angry with yourselves, that ye sold me hither" (Genesis 45:5a).

Read 1 John 1:3–7.

Note. To read the story of Joseph's life of slavery and how he rose to power, read Genesis 39–41.

1. Why can we not have true fellowship with God if we have hidden sins?

_____

2. Other than fellowship with God, what are two benefits of walking in the light? _____

_____

_____

Read Luke 12:2–3 and 1 John 2:8–10 to answer questions 3–6.

3. What are the consequences of not walking in the light? _____

_____

_____

4. What are two signs that we are still in darkness? _____

_____

_____

5. Other than anger, what are some ways that hidden sin causes stumbling?

_____

_____

6. How does the darkness blind our eyes? _____

_____

Fellowship = companionship, communion, intimate familiarity

Read 1 John 1:8–9 and James 5:16 to answer questions 7–9.

7. What must we do if we are to be without any sin? _____

_____

8. How do we bring our sin to the light? _____

_____

9. In this study, what is one purpose given for confessing our sins and walking in the light? _____

_____

_____

"Ye were called unto the fellowship of his Son Jesus Christ our Lord"
 (1 Corinthians 1:9b).

Walking in the light will eliminate a source of anger, but the real goal of transparency is fellowship with the Lord Jesus Christ and with your heavenly Father. Seek intimacy with the Lord. Any intimate relationship needs to be nurtured. Spend time with Him. Bare your heart to Him. Listen to Him. He has paid the price in order to have intimate fellowship with you. Do not miss the opportunity.

Pray a commitment to God from what you have learned.

Digging Deeper:

Isaiah 2:5	Isaiah 50:10
Luke 1:78–79	John 3:20–21
John 11:10	1 Corinthians 4:5
Ephesians 5:8–10	Isaiah 29:15
Micah 7:7–8	Psalm 66:18
Psalm 32:1	Psalm 51:1–4

15 Maintain Your Mind

"Among whom also we all had our conversation in times past in the lusts of our flesh, fulfilling the desires of the flesh and of the mind; and were by nature the children of wrath, even as others?" (Ephesians 2:3).

Read Ephesians 2:1–10.

We are quick to see that fleshly desires that lead to immorality are wrong. We also recognize that people who fulfill such desires suffer consequences such as broken relationships, separated families, and lost jobs. We're not surprised that these people are called the children of wrath. However, desires of the mind also have dire consequences. They are just as significant as the desires of the flesh in their effect on our relationships.

We've been told that it's a sin to look at another person (or at pictures of another) with lustful thoughts. Here, we see that it is also harmful to entertain such thoughts in our minds. We need to guard our minds, because the enemy gains a foothold in our hearts and lives through our minds.

God desires purity in our hearts. When we entertain lustful thoughts, we open the door for pollution in our hearts. As a consequence, we are no longer able to relate openly and freely with God.

What are these desires of our minds? What do we lust for? Do we not sometimes lust after power? Popularity? Prestige? Material comforts? Food, alcohol, cigarettes, or drugs? Immoral stimulation? There is a disease in our land—a disease that entices us to desire things that are newer, bigger, better, prettier, more powerful, or more stimulating.

With false hopes of gaining satisfaction or fulfillment, people throw sensibility and responsibility aside and entangle themselves in debt and deception in order to fulfill desires. Laws and relationships are disregarded in order to obtain the desired items.

Maintain
Your Mind

Many in the church are just as caught up in temporal pursuits as those who do not know Jesus Christ. This should not be so. This verse reveals that if we continue to pursue such desires, we will be children of wrath; we will remain angry.

Even when indulged, temporal, fleshly desires will never bring true satisfaction. They are focused on self, and will lead to discontentment, dissatisfaction, and anger.

The lasting satisfaction and fulfillment that we are seeking come from things that are eternal. Only as we seek the kingdom of God and His righteousness will we find fulfillment for the longing in our hearts.

Pray: Ask the Lord to examine your heart and reveal to you any area in which the desires of your mind are not pleasing to Him. Commit yourself to guard your mind and no longer to lust after the things of the world. Commit your life to be focused on God and others—not yourself.

15 Maintain Your Mind

Application of Ephesians 2:3

"Among whom also we all had our conversation in times past in the lusts of our flesh, fulfilling the desires of the flesh and of the mind; and were by nature the children of wrath, even as others" (Ephesians 2:3).

Read Matthew 6:19–25.

1. How do verses 19–21 relate to verses 22–23? _____

_____

1b. How do they all relate to verses 24–25? _____

_____

2. According to Ephesians 2:3, those who lust for the desires of the flesh/mind are angry. From these verses in Matthew, can you deduce what would cause them to be angry? _____

_____

Check the areas that relate to your personal struggle with fleshly desires in your mind.

_____ Material goods (clothes/house/car/things)

_____ Popularity/to be liked

_____ Prestige/power/ to be "somebody" or be respected

_____Talents/intelligence/beauty

_____ Immorality (be specific about nature of struggle)

_____ Other

Read Matthew 6:26–34.

3. What is the cure for anger that springs from lustful desires?_____

_____

4. What are one or two specific things that you can do today to seek first His kingdom and righteousness? _____

_____

Pray. Confess the sin of putting yourself and other things before God. (Be specific, from the list above.) Commit to make God the center of your life. Ask Him to create a new heart within you.

"I made a covenant with mine eyes: why then should I think upon a maid?" (Job 31:1).

Frequently, temptation to lust enters the mind through the doorway of the eyes. If you make a covenant with your eyes to not look upon (lingering or looking back) the things that tempt you (whether it be a person, food, or things), the battle in the mind will be lessened. Be diligent to guard your eyes and your thoughts so they will not seek to fulfill your fleshly desires.

Pray. Job made a covenant with his eyes. Do you wish to make a similar commitment to God? _____

_____

_____

Digging Deeper:
2 Corinthians 10:5   Romans 12:2
Ephesians 4:20–24   Philippians 4:11–13
1 Timothy 6:8   Proverbs 30:8
Luke 9:62

16 Smug and Self-Sufficient

"Then Asa was wroth with the seer, and put him in a prison house; for he was in a rage with him" (2 Chronicles 16:10).

Read 2 Chronicles 15:1–16:14.

Asa was King of Judah and he "did that which was good and right in the eyes of the LORD his God" (2 Chron. 14:2). He tore down idols and commanded Judah to follow God. When attacked, he cried out to God for help.

In response, God blessed Asa with fifteen years of peace in the land. Asa loved the Lord and tried to lead the nation to follow God, so why, in 2 Chronicles 16:10, did Asa get angry with the seer sent from God and throw him in prison?

During all those years of peace, when things were going well, Asa forgot that God was shield and protector to His children. Consequently, when Judah was attacked by Israel, Asa chose to look to Syria instead of calling on God for aid. A seer confronted Asa about relying on Syria, rather than relying on God. He said, "Thou hast done foolishly: therefore from henceforth thou shalt have wars" (2 Chron. 16:9b).

Asa responded in anger. He put the seer in prison and began to oppress some of his own people because of the seer's words!

When things are going well, we, like Asa, often become smug and let our relationship with God slip. We forget that our blessings come from the Lord. Consequently, we arrogantly act as if there is no God, take care of our own problems, and seek help from those around us—rather than seeking God.

If we react in anger when confronted, it's a warning sign that things are not right in our hearts. If we, like Asa, fail to repent, we can expect future wars in our lives. On the other hand, if we repent, it will lead to restoration of fellowship with God and thus to peace in our lives.

Smug and
Self-Sufficient

We do have a choice. The next time we are confronted, we need to pause and think of the consequences before reacting in anger. Maybe, like Asa, we have forgotten our God.

Pray: Confess to God if you've become smug and self-sufficient or have reacted to confrontations. Ask Him to help you to rely on Him at all times and to help you humble yourself to receive correction and repent when it is needed.

16 Smug and Self-Sufficient

Application of 2 Chronicles 16:10

"Then Asa was wroth with the seer, and put him in a prison house; for he was in a rage with him" (2 Chronicles 16:10).

Answer the questions below, considering how the truths of Romans 1:21–22 (in margin) can be seen in Asa's life as it is related to us in 2 Chronicles 15:1–16:14. The numbers inserted in parentheses (in the Romans passage) refer to the numbers of the questions below.

"Because that, when (1) they knew God, (2) they glorified him not as God, (4) neither were thankful; but (5) became vain in their imaginations, and (6) their foolish heart was darkened. (7) Professing them-selves to be wise, they became fools" (Romans 1:21–22, numbers and parentheses added).

1. How does the story of Asa show that he knew God? _____

_____

2. Did Asa glorify God as God in chapter 15? In chapter 16? Explain.

_____

_____

3. How is God glorified when we call on Him? _____

_____

4. Is there evidence that Asa was thankful? _____

_____

5. What evidence is there that he became vain in his imaginations?

_____

6. Is there evidence that Asa's heart was darkened?_____

_____

7. How did he act like a fool? _____

_____

Consider your life:

8. In what areas are you tempted to be smug and self-sufficient?

   _____

   _____

9. When corrected, what is your normal response?

   _____

   _____

10. Have you been vain (empty or foolish) in your imaginations (thoughts)? _____

11. Has your heart been darkened (dark and confused)? _____

Read Romans 1:24, 28, and Romans 2:5.

12. In the book of Romans, according to the Apostle Paul, what are the consequences for knowing God but failing to honor Him as God?

    _____

    _____

Pray. If you have been self-sufficient and complacent, repent and ask God to forgive you. Ask Him to restore to you the joy of fellowship with Him.

Digging Deeper.

Proverbs 29:1
Proverbs 10:17
Proverbs 13:18
2 Corinthians 7:10

Proverbs 1:24–26
2 Chronicles 36:15–16
2 Timothy 3:16–17

17 My Way

"And when Haman saw that Mordecai bowed not, nor did him reverence, then was Haman full of wrath" (Esther 3:5).

Read Esther 2:1–3:6. (For the whole fascinating story, read the book of Esther.)

Haman's proud, self-centered scheming could make us rejoice that he ended up being hanged (Est. 7:1–10). However, if we would pause and look at our own angry outbursts, we might find the same attitudes. Am I often angry because I don't get what I want? Do I try to manipulate things to go my way? The expectation to get my way is rooted in pride and self-centeredness. Could a bit of Haman be in me?

Not all pride is as flagrant as Haman's, but any time we are focused on ourselves, we are walking in pride. Whether considering how good we are, how bad we are, or how much we've been hurt, in all of these, the common element is that we are focused on SELF; we are seeking the desires of self, rather than of God.

When we seek our own way, we can't seek to please God at the same time. (Sometimes we do seek to walk in His way, but then we proceed in self-centeredness, trying to walk out His purposes in our own strength!)

When self is thwarted, we react, defiling all those around us. Whether it is expressed in an explosion, in sullen silence, or in calculating coolness, our reaction is anger, and it does not accomplish our goal in the long run. Even when our anger does achieve the response we want, we fail to see that the response is only external.

The hearts of those around us close toward us, respect and authority are lost, and the next time it will take more anger to accomplish our desires. The pattern escalates, building toward destruction—the promised reward for pride—and the inevitable consequence of anger (Prov. 16:18).

We don't have to be like Haman. However, if we continue to expect to always get what we want (things going our way), our pride will also

My Way

lead to our fall. We cannot righteously expect others to bow down to our desires.

Pray: Ask God to reveal your pride and self-centeredness to you. Confess your sin of pride, and ask Him to teach you to be humble in spirit.

17 My Way

Application of Esther 3:5

> *"And when Haman saw that Mordecai bowed not, nor did him reverence, then was Haman full of wrath"* (Esther 3:5).

Read the following Scriptures. List the truth about pride that you learn from each passage.

1. Mark 7:21–23 _____

2. 1 Peter 3:12, 5:5 _____

3. Proverbs 16:18–19 _____

4. Proverbs 8:13 _____

5. In Mark 7:20–23 note the things Jesus groups with pride. _____

_____

_____

6. Which of the following pride indicators do you exhibit?

___Not listening to others   ___Expecting your way

___Excessive talking   ___Always knowing the answer

___Not forgiving   ___Self-pity/Self-conscious

___Noticing when others fail   ___Desiring success/Recognition

___Quick to assign blame   ___Independent/Self-sufficient

___Hides own sins   ___Concerned about what others think

My Way

The remedy for pride is recognizing what others, and ultimately God, have contributed to your life, and how little you deserve what you have.

Summarize the verses below in your own words.

7. Proverbs 29:23 _____

_____

8. James 1:17 _____

_____

9. John 15:5 _____

_____

10. James 4:6, 10 _____

_____

What do you hear God saying to you? _____

_____

Pray: Respond to God from your heart.

Digging Deeper:

Psalm 37:11	Psalm 138:6
Proverbs 22:4	Matthew 11:29
Mark 9:33–37	Luke 14:7–14
Luke 22:24–27	John 13:14–16
Romans 12:3, 10, 16	1 Corinthians 10:12
1 Corinthians 13:4	Philippians 2:3–11

18 Don't You Care?

"But Martha was encumbered about much serving, and came to him, and said, Lord, dost thou not care that my sister hath left me to serve alone? bid her therefore that she help me" (Luke 10:40).

Read Luke 10:38–42.

Can't you hear Martha's irritation as she asked, "Jesus, don't you care that my sister has left all the work to me?" She would have to be pretty stressed and frustrated with her sister before she would interrupt Jesus with the question, "Don't you care?" I can imagine Martha defending herself: "I wasn't angry! I was frustrated!" However, the people around her would have heard anger in her voice.

Martha is often perceived as being less spiritual than her sister Mary, because Martha was in the kitchen instead of sitting at Jesus' feet. However, other stories in the Bible show us that she loved Jesus too. It was out of this love that she was preparing a meal for Him. She also had a special relationship with Him, or she would not have felt free to come to Him in her frustration/anger.

Jesus' response to Martha directs us to the issues that are important in our lives when we are frustrated. Jesus answered, "Martha, Martha." (Do you hear the tender caring in His response?) "Thou art careful and troubled about many things: But one thing is needful: and Mary hath chosen that good part, which shall not be taken away from her" (vv. 41–42).

The difference between Martha and Mary is obvious. Mary saw nothing but Jesus when He entered the room. Her whole attention was on Him. She chose Jesus, rather than service to Jesus. Martha loved Jesus and was very aware of him, but like the seed that is choked out by the cares of the day (described in Luke 8) Martha was distracted by her service.

Many of us are like Martha. We love Jesus and seek to serve Him, but things distract us. The "cares, riches, and pleasures of this life" choke us and we "bring no fruit to perfection" (Luke 8:14). We may carry what seems like more than our share of the load. Frustration builds, leading to anger toward someone nearby.

We then come to God with our complaints against the other person — but the problem is in our own heart, not with the other person. We've allowed demands and cares to choke out a relationship with our Lord. Jesus does care. He is longing for an intimate relationship with us. If we will take the time to seek His face, we'll find grace to respond right-eously when we are under pressure.

Pray. Confess and ask the Lord to forgive you for your lack of adoration and your many distractions. Seek God for how to make time to sit at His feet and for discipline to carry it out.

18 Don't You Care?

Application of Luke 10:40

"But Martha was encumbered about much serving, and came to him, and said, Lord, dost thou not care that my sister hath left me to serve alone? bid her therefore that she help me" (Luke 10:40).

Read Luke 8:4–15.

1. What did Jesus say is referred to by the seed that is sown?

_____

2. What happens to the seed sown beside the road? _____

_____

3. What is the result in the lives of those people?_____

_____

4. Which seed would represent your life if you are constantly distracted, as Martha was distracted when Jesus visited? _____

_____

5. According to Jesus, what things distract us? What are the consequences of that distraction? _____

_____

_____

6. What happens to the seed that falls on the good soil? How was Martha's anxiety and distraction robbing her?

_____

_____

Read Philippians 4:6–7.

7. What four things does Paul mention that we need to do when we become anxious about people or distractions in life?_____

_____

_____

Note: The words *prayer, supplication* (petition), and *request* are similar in meaning, even in the Greek; three of the four words say basically the same thing. The word for *prayer* includes the idea of worship, and the word for *request* includes the idea of begging, but all three words would draw our attention back to the Lord. Martha did that. She went to the Lord; BUT she lacked the fourth element. When we are anxious, we are to go to the Lord "with thanksgiving."

8. Ask the Lord to search your heart and reveal what your reactions are when you find yourself in Martha's situation.

_____

_____

9. When have you been in a situation similar to Martha's when you got angry?

_____

_____

10. What would God have you do differently? _____

_____

_____

_____

_____

Note: Answers will vary, depending on the situation. Seek God's will.

Pray: Surrender to the Lord the thing you are anxious about, asking Him for grace to deal with it according to His will. Ask God to help you commit to do only the things He has prepared for you to do. Ask God to forgive you for being anxious, for not seeking Him first, and for not seeking Him with thanksgiving when you are stressed. Ask that your life be full of fruit for the kingdom of God.

When we give things to God, we tend to pick them up again. You may need to pray this prayer every day or even several times a day. Memorize Philippians 4:6–7 and meditate on it as a reminder.

Digging Deeper:

Matthew 11:28–30

Psalm 105:1

1 Thessalonians 5:15–18

2 Corinthians 9:8

Psalm 9:9–10

Colossians 3:14–17

Romans 8:6–8

Romans 14:17–19

1 Corinthians 3:13–15

19 Who Is on the Throne?

"But it displeased Jonah exceedingly, and he was very angry"
(Jonah 4:1).

Read Jonah 1:1–4:11.

God handpicked Jonah for a job, but Jonah chose to run away rather than obey God. Even though God dramatically intervened in Jonah's circumstances, Jonah remained focused on himself. When God was merciful to Nineveh, Jonah became angry. The outcome Jonah expected and his reputation were more important to him than the salvation of Nineveh!

Like Jonah, we often fail to recognize the sovereign hand of God at work in our lives. We, too, are affected by the people around us, by our expectations, or by the lack of desired comforts. If, like Jonah, we become consumed with our needs and our desires, we become frustrated and angry when things don't go our way. In essence, we place ourselves on the throne of our lives.

When we hold onto our rights and expectations and try to make our lives like we want them to be, we are denying the lordship of God, and we can be sure He will resist the pride in us. In His kingdom, God sits on the throne. If He is not on the throne of our lives, we will not enjoy the benefits of His kingdom, including His righteousness, peace, and joy.

We cannot live for ourselves and for God at the same time. We must choose whether to hold onto our rights or to yield our lives to God. When we get angry at others for infringing on our rights, it is really God whom we are fighting. The more we demand our own way and resist Him, the more we experience frustrations and anger. As we can see in Jonah's life, the Lord sometimes allows us to go our own way for a while, but with God as our opponent, we will not win the battle.

Pray. Repent of your lack of submission to God's lordship. Ask Him to search your heart and shine His light on the areas in which you resist Him. Give all your desires and expectations to Him. Commit to live your life for Him, rather than seeking your own way.

19 Who Is on the Throne?

Application of Jonah 4:1

"But it displeased Jonah exceedingly, and he was very angry"
(Jonah 4:1).

Read Exodus 20:2–3 and Matthew 6:24.

1. How does seeking your own way rather than God's way violate the command found in Exodus 20:3? _____
_____

2. If you continue to seek your own way, serving your desires, what will that do to your relationship with God? _____
_____

3. How will that affect your relationship with other people? _____
_____

4. In what area (or under what circumstances) do you resist yielding your rights? _____
_____
_____

Read Genesis 13:1–18.

5. What was the point of strife and contention? _____
_____
_____

6. Who had the right to choose? Where did he get the right? _____

_____

_____

7. Why would Abram yield his right to Lot? _____

_____

8. Looking at the situation with natural eyes, would it seem fair?

_____

9. Was God faithful to care for and provide for Abram? _____

10. Are you willing, like Abram, to trust God to care for you and pro-
    vide for you? _____

11. List the things that are the most difficult for you to give up to God.

_____

_____

_____

Pray: Yield your rights to God, placing your trust in Him for your care, protection, and provision. Be specific in giving Him the things that you have the greatest difficulty giving up. Give Him the things you have listed in #11.

Read John 12:24–26.

12. If we die to ourselves and our own rights, what can we expect?

_____

_____

_____

Relinquish your rights.
Let God choose
for you.

13. Compare the things you listed in #11 and the things promised in these verses (fruitfulness, eternal life, being honored by God). Which do you want for your life—things listed or the things promised by God?

Jesus said, "I seek not mine own will, but the will of the Father which hath sent me" (John 5:30b).

Pray. Thank God for the life you have in Him. Give Him anything you are still holding onto and ask Him to help you live your life surrendered to His will.

Digging Deeper:

Romans 14:11

Matthew 7:21

1 Samuel 15:22

Psalm 18:30–33

Psalm 36:7–9

1 John 5:3

Matthew 12:50

Psalm 37:5–7

Psalm 31:19–21

20 Stopped Again?

"And when the ass saw the angel of the Lord, she fell down under Balaam: and Balaam's anger was kindled, and he smote the ass with a staff" (Numbers 22:27).

Read Numbers 22:1–34.

(For the full story of Balaam, read Numbers 22–24.)

Balaam was angry because an obstacle prevented him from achieving his goal. He didn't stop to consider that the donkey had never balked before or that maybe God had a hand in the delay. His mind was on his goal, and he was frustrated by the interruption.

How often do we get angry because our agenda is hindered or stopped? We learn to set goals to be successful in life, and we measure success by their completion. However, we fail to consider how much frustration and anger we experience because of the pressure to achieve. We also fail to realize that in pursuing our goals we might be missing God's goals for us.

Balaam made two mistakes. First, achieving his personal goals was more important to him than obeying God. God had made His wishes known, but Balaam followed man's voice rather than God's.

Secondly, as God tried to get Balaam's attention, Balaam still thought only of his own goal. God promises to direct our paths if we acknowledge Him in all our ways, but Balaam did not acknowledge God at all.

God uses many attention-getters: a person, an illness, an accident, a traumatic loss, traffic, or such. If our reaction to the interference is to become frustrated and angry, God has three options: (1) He can smash us for our rebellion and independence, (2) He can leave us to go our own way and allow us to reap the inevitable negative consequences, or (3) He can have mercy upon us and put more hindrances in our path!

Stopped Again?

If we focus on our own agenda, we see all of these acts of God as opposition to progress. Consequently, we miss the guiding hand of God!

Goals are not bad—they help us establish purpose and become productive. But we need balance. We need to seek first God's kingdom and His righteousness (Matt. 6:33). Our focus needs to be on God and eternal matters, not on what we want. As we pursue our goals, if we're acknowledging God, we'll recognize His voice, and He can direct and adjust our path.

Pray. Repent for putting your own agenda above God's, for not listening for His direction, and for not heeding His correction. Commit your ways to God. Surrender your life to His lordship.

20 Stopped Again?

Application of Numbers 22:27

"And when the ass saw the angel of the LORD, she fell down under Balaam: and Balaam's anger was kindled, and he smote the ass with a staff" (Numbers 22:27).

Read John 12:25–26.

Decide: Which do you want? Your agenda and goals ___ or God's goals for you ___?

Look up the following verses and summarize the message from each:

Proverbs 14:12 _____

_____

Proverbs 14:14 _____

_____

Proverbs 16:2 _____

_____

Psalm 139:16 _____

_____

Ephesians 2:10 _____

_____

"In all thy ways acknowledge him, and he shall direct thy paths" (Prov. 3:6).

The Scriptures give us many examples of people who were directed by God. What did God use to change the direction of each one listed below?

Moses (Ex. 3): _____

_____

Stopped Again?

Joseph (Gen. 37:11, 23–28): _____
_____

Gideon (Jud. 6–7): _____
_____

David (1 Sam. 16:1–13, 17:17, 18:7–9): _____
_____

Saul (Acts 9:1–9): _____
_____

Believers (Acts 8:3–4): _____
_____

Peter (Acts 10:9–23): _____
_____

(Notice that when our heroes of faith did not follow God's new direction immediately, the Lord did not become impatient with them if they were seeking confirmation that He was speaking.)

Three options: God can respond in three different ways if we don't obey Him:

1. The Lord can smash us for our rebellion and independence.

   Proverbs 29:1 _____

   2 Chronicles 36:15–16 _____

2. God can leave us to go our own way and allow us to reap the inevitable negative consequences.

   Romans 1:18–25 (especially v. 21) _____

   Proverbs 1:24–33 _____

3. God can have mercy upon us and put more hindrances in our path.

John 1:14–17 _____

Joshua 7 _____

Exodus 7–12 _____

Acts 13:50–51 _____

Acts 14:5–7 _____

4. Which of the three responses have you experienced? Did you recognize the hand of God in each situation? _____

_____

_____

5. Did you respond in anger? What would you do differently today? _____

_____

_____

Seek first the kingdom of God. Let Him direct your life!

Pray. Ask God to forgive you for the times you responded in anger. Ask God to strengthen you to be quick to see Him in all circumstances and quick to follow Him.

Digging Deeper.

Proverbs 29:1

Isaiah 40:11

Isaiah 42:6

Isaiah 45:12–13

Proverbs 8:32–36

Jeremiah 26:3–6

Romans 1:18–24

Jeremiah 10:23–24

21 Who's Boss?

"Now it came about that when Sanballat heard that we were rebuilding the wall, he became furious and very angry and mocked the Jews. . . . Now it came about when Sanballat, Tobiah, the Arabs, the Ammonites, and the Ashdodites heard that the repair of the walls of Jerusalem went on, and that the breaches began to be closed, they were very angry" (Nehemiah 4:1, 7, NASB).

Read Nehemiah 1:1–2:2 and 4:1–9.

We sometimes get angry with those who are doing God's will, just as Sanballat became angry when Nehemiah was rebuilding the walls of Jerusalem. Sanballat was fearful because a city within his jurisdiction was being fortified. It seemed he would lose control. He reacted in anger that was accompanied by mockery and verbal attacks (v. 1), by slander and gossip (v. 2), and by gathering reinforcements to join him in coming against Jerusalem (vv. 7–8).

Because they fear loss, many people become angry when they (like Sanballat) sense that their authority is being threatened. Anger gives us a sense of power, which we use to try to maintain control. Like Sanballat, we sometimes even influence others around us in an attempt to further insure our authority. Such tactics indicate a lack of understanding of the nature of authority and control.

Sanballat was the legitimate ruler of the region, but he and Nehemiah were both under the king's authority. The king granted Nehemiah permission to oversee the rebuilding of Jerusalem, so as Sanballat opposed Nehemiah, he was also opposing the king. Sanballat was looking out for his own good, not for that of the king or of those in his territory. Righteous authority represents those above them while seeking to serve those under them.

Sanballat was also taking it upon himself to maintain his control. He did not realize that all authority is from God. Neither did he realize that he did not need to enforce his authority because God would maintain it for him. If Sanballat had helped Nehemiah complete his goal, he would have gained the respect and loyalty of the whole city.

Instead, by opposing Nehemiah, he placed himself in opposition to God. Through his attempts to maintain control, Sanballat only made matters worse. By opposing someone under his authority, he ended up in opposition to the king and to the Lord!

The control gained through anger brings more harm than good. Anger does not produce the righteousness of God and thus does not maintain godly authority. We do not need to strive to maintain authority. As we seek God and seek to serve those around us, He will maintain our position of authority for us.

Pray. Repent of seeking to enforce control and for lack of trust in God. Yield your life to God, including specific people or situations with whom you are struggling. Allow Him to maintain control for you.

21 Who's Boss?

Application of Nehemiah 4:1

"Now it came about that when Sanballat heard that we were rebuilding the wall, he became furious and very angry and mocked the Jews" (Nehemiah 4:1, NASB).

Read Luke 22:24–27.

1. How does Jesus describe the way the Gentiles (unbelievers) lead?

_____

2. Is that how Jesus wants us to lead? How do you know? _____

_____

_____

Note: A benefactor is "one who does good."[4] Jesus is recognizing that not everything that is done by one who has authority and lords it over another is bad. However, he continues by challenging our ideas of greatness, of leadership, and of our goal as Christians.

3. What did Jesus say about the one who leads or is greatest? _____

_____

_____

4. If someone lords it over you, does it:

___ Get the job done?   ___ Train you for the job?

___ Make you obey?   ___ Win loyalty?

___ Win respect?   ___ Build character?

___ Draw you to the Lord?   ___ Build your relationship
                                   with your boss?

Who's Boss?

Note: A centurion is a captain who has authority over a military unit of one hundred men.[5]

Place an X beside items below that indicate how it makes you feel when someone lords it over you. Place a check beside the ones that show how you want people to feel in response to you.

___ Cheerfully willing   ___ Pushed, manipulated

___ Confident   ___ Demanded

___ Valued, appreciated   ___ Resistant

___ Like a team player   ___ Used

___ Other

Read Matthew 8:5–10.

5. In verse 9, what did the centurion identify as his source of authority, which caused his commands to be followed? _____

_____

6. After such a short interchange of words, what did Jesus say about the centurion? _____

_____

7. How did the centurion demonstrate faith? _____

_____

Read Romans 13:1–7 and 2 Corinthians 10:8.

8. Why should we obey our authority? _____

_____

9. If we resist authority, whom are we opposing? _____

_____

10. Why did God establish authority? _____

_____

11. How was Sanballat unrighteous in his use of authority?

_____

_____

12. What could he have done differently?

_____

_____

The keys to righteous authority illustrated in these passages are:

    1) Faith in the Lord, the One who places people in authority

    2) Representing those above you

    3) Serving those under you for their good

Pray: Anger is a tool for lording it over others. Repent of times when you have used anger to maintain control, and ask God to teach you to look to Him and trust Him as He teaches you to handle authority righteously.

Digging Deeper:

To learn about people who trusted God to maintain their authority during adversity, read the following passages.

    Joseph: Genesis 37:1–33, 39:1–41:46

    Esther: Esther 2–7

    Daniel: Daniel 1:5–20, 2:46–49, 6:1–28

    David: 1 Samuel 16:1–13, 18:7–19:17, 23:13–24:22, 26:1–24

    Jesus: Luke 22–23

    Prayer of trust: Psalm 59

22 All for a Vineyard?

"And Ahab came into his house heavy and displeased because of the word which Naboth the Jezreelite had spoken to him: for he had said, I will not give thee the inheritance of my fathers. And he laid him down upon his bed, and turned away his face, and would eat no bread" (1 Kings 21:4).

Read 1 Kings 21:1–29.

Ahab was angry because he could not have the vineyard allotted to Naboth by God. Naboth dared to say no to the king, saying, "God forbid that I should give mine inheritance to thee" (v. 3). As king, Ahab was used to getting what he wanted. Rather than acknowledge God's authority in the allotment of territory, he continued to lust for Naboth's land.

Ahab's greed led to anger, and he sulked and refused to eat. Jezebel, not wanting to see her husband sulk, did the dirty work to get the vineyard for him. She borrowed Ahab's authority and had Naboth killed on false charges! Ahab's sulking and anger led to the fulfillment of his desire, but it also led to the judgment of God on him and his wife.

Even though he knew nothing about Jezebel's scheme to kill Naboth, God held Ahab responsible for the murder. He told Elijah to go to Ahab and pronounce his punishment as soon as Ahab went down to claim the vineyard. Elijah's words to Ahab were, "Hast *thou* killed, and also taken possession?" (v. 19, italics added).

The consequences of murdering Naboth were sudden and dramatic. Ahab was killed, and the dogs licked his blood in the same place that they had licked Naboth's! The dogs also ate Jezebel by the wall of Jezreel (vv. 19, 23).

We may not be in the position of king, but we often adopt the attitude of Ahab, especially if we have been given authority—no matter how small that authority is. Like Ahab, when we manipulate others with anger, ultimately we lose. The final consequences of greed, anger, and manipulation outweigh the prize we gain. Ahab did not come to

All for a
Vineyard?

destruction because of a vineyard; it was a greedy heart—expressed in sullen anger—that led to his death.

Pray: Confess greed, anger, and manipulation. Ask God to show you if there are any "vineyards" in your life. Commit to seek first His kingdom and His righteousness.

22 All for a Vineyard?

Application of 1 Kings 21:4

*"And Ahab came into his house heavy and displeased . . . .
And he laid him down upon his bed, and turned away his
face, and would eat no bread"* (1 Kings 21:4).

Read Matthew 6:19–34.

1. From the verses below, list reasons to overcome greed.

v. 19 _____

v. 21 _____

vv. 22–23 _____

v. 24 _____

v. 25 _____

v. 26 _____

v. 27 _____

vv. 28–30 _____

v. 32 _____

v. 33 _____

v. 34 _____

2. *Key Verse:* Which of these verses is the key verse, the one that best
   summarizes what God is saying to you? Summarize it in your own
   words. _____

   _____

   _____

Pray: Take a moment to respond to God from your heart.

3. Read and summarize Matthew 7:7–11. _____

   _____

   _____

4. Read and summarize James 4:3–4. _____
_____
_____

5. Considering the passages studied, how would you counsel Ahab to help him overcome his anger? _____
_____

Describe the problem: _____
_____

The solution: _____
_____

Pray: Confess to God the times you have not sought Him for provision and have been manipulative to get what you wanted.

Digging Deeper:

Exodus 20:17   Luke 12:15
Colossians 3:5–6   Ecclesiastes 5:10–11
Philippians 4:11   Hebrews 13:5
1 Timothy 6:6–12   Ephesians 5:3–5
1 John 2:15   Proverbs 30:8–9
Proverbs 21:25–26   2 Corinthians 9:6–7

23 Jealousy

"Now Eliab his oldest brother heard when he spoke to the men; and Eliab's anger burned against David and he said, 'Why have you come down? And with whom have you left those few sheep in the wilderness? I know your insolence and the wickedness of your heart; for you have come down in order to see the battle' " (1 Samuel 17:28, NASB).

Read 1 Samuel 17:1–58.

For forty days, the Philistine giant, Goliath, had terrified the army of Israel with his confrontations. David saw that the taunt hurled at the people of God by an "uncircumcised Philistine" was actually a challenge issued to the living God.

David was not filled with fear as the other men were, because he had seen the Lord's faithfulness in crises, and he was confident in God. When Eliab recognized the faith and confidence in God that were expressed in the questions of his little brother, he became jealous and angry toward David.

Jealousy leads us to seek ways to tear down and discredit the other person. Often, as with Eliab, those accusations are likely a better description of ourselves than of the one with whom we are angry. Even if the accusation is not spoken, if the spirit of accusation is in us, the relationship is harmed. The old maxim that it takes a pot to call a kettle black has some truth to it. Eliab accused David of irresponsibility, pride, and an unclean heart.

When we compare ourselves to others, we often feel that someone else is getting what we deserve (whether recognition, position, or material things). Because we reason that we are as deserving as the other person, we then become angry, feeling that we have been slighted. If we look to man for our reward rather than looking to God, we will often become hurt and jealous.

God is sovereign. He raises up and puts down. The king's heart is in His hands. His love for us is perfect, so we can trust Him for what is best

Jealousy

in our lives. Rather than looking to those around us for approval and worth, we can trust Him for our reward.

As we look to God (instead of to others), not only will we be free of jealousy, but we also will be filled with His righteousness, peace, and joy. We will then have the grace to respond without anger.

Pray: Repent of comparing yourself with others and for looking to man for your reward. Ask God to help you to trust Him, and to look to Him, rather than looking to man for approval and affirmation.

23 Jealousy

Application of 1 Samuel 17:28

". . . And Eliab's anger burned against David and he said, 'Why have you come down? . . . I know your insolence and the wickedness of your heart; for you have come down in order to see the battle'" (1 Samuel 17:28, NASB).

Read Romans 12:1–2.

1. When an animal is sacrificed, what percentage of the animal dies?

   _____

2. When you present your body as a living sacrifice, what percentage can you hold for yourself? _____

3. If you are a living sacrifice, what dies? _____

4. To determine if you have died (surrendered to God), ask the following questions about your daily life:

   ✳ Are you willing to do whatever God asks—for His glory, even with no recognition?

   ✳ Do you compare your value (or value of deeds done) to that of others?

   ✳ Do you serve without grumbling or complaining?

   ✳ Do you look to God or to man for your reward (recognition)?

5. According to the questions above, have you died to self and surrendered your life to God for His purposes and His glory? _____

   _____

We are able to look to God for our reward, rather than to man, only to the degree that we have surrendered our lives to Him.

Jealousy

6. If your answer to #5 is yes, and you still suffer from jealousy, ask yourself, "Have I left the sacrifice on the altar?" _____

When you surrender to God for His purposes, you will learn to walk in joy wherever He leads you, and you will learn to be content, trusting Him for direction and reward.

Another problem with Eliab, and with us, could be anger against God for honoring someone else. As long as the anger against God remains in our hearts, we will have a problem with jealousy and anger toward others.

Read Isaiah 64:8, Romans 9:21, and Jeremiah 18:2–6.

7. How does the analogy of the potter and clay apply to God and to us?

_____

_____

8. How well can we comprehend the purposes of God?

_____

_____

9. Can we know the best way to bring about His purposes in a given situation? _____

_____

Pray: Repent of any attempts to tell God how it ought to be, and yield your life into the Potter's hands.

Digging Deeper:

Philippians 2:3   Psalm 75:5–7

1 Samuel 2:7–8   2 Corinthians 10:5, 12, 18

24 Listen to Yourself!

"Then Saul's anger was kindled against Jonathan, and he said unto him, Thou son of the perverse rebellious woman, do not I know that thou hast chosen the son of Jesse to thine own confusion, and unto the confusion of thy mother's nakedness?" (1 Samuel 20:30).

Read 1 Samuel 18:1–16, 28–29.

Saul's words of anger were directed at his son, Jonathan, but his primary anger was against David. Saul was jealous of David—of his success in battle, of the people's admiration of him, of God's favor upon him, and of his own son's loyalty to him.

Jealousy, left unchecked, grows and grows. It is like a cancer that feeds on anything around and grows out of control. Jealousy then leads to bitterness, wrath, anger, and attitudes that would not be allowed to continue in a righteous heart. The anger is often directed toward other people rather than the object of the jealousy.

If Saul tried to control his anger toward Jonathan, he would be fighting a losing battle without first dealing with his jealousy and anger toward David. We can see in 1 Samuel 18:28–29 that Saul's jealousy toward David was actually rooted in rebellion toward God: "And Saul saw and knew that the Lord was with David . . . and Saul was yet the more afraid of David; and Saul became David's enemy continually."

If Saul were "with God," he would have no reason to fear David, because God was "with David"! Because Saul was in rebellion against God, he feared when he saw God's hand upon David. The accusation he hurls at Jonathan pinpoints the root of his own problem of rebellion: "Thou son of the perverse rebellious woman" (1 Sam. 20:30). Saul was the one who was perverse and rebellious. We, like Saul, often label others with the sin that we are guilty of.

When we are angry, if we would listen to the accusations we hurl at others (whether we say them or just think them in our hearts), we could often discover the root of our anger problem. As with Saul, the problem is usually a problem between me and God, more than a problem between me and the other person.

Pray. Ask God to search your heart for rebellion and jealousy. Ask Him to forgive you for judging others, for anger, for jealousy, and for rebellion. Commit to walk with God rather than in rebellion against Him. Ask Him to renew a right spirit in you, so that you would be pleasing in His sight.

24 Listen to Yourself!

Application of 1 Samuel 20:30

"Then Saul's anger was kindled against Jonathan, and he said unto him, 'Thou son of the perverse rebellious woman, do not I know that thou hast chosen the son of Jesse to thine own confusion, and unto the confusion of thy mother's nakedness?'" (1 Samuel 20:30).

Read 1 Samuel 15 to discover the root of Saul's jealousy and anger.

1. What are God's instructions to Saul? (vv. 3–9) _____

_____

2. Did Saul obey? _____

3. What is the response of God, and of Samuel, to Saul's actions? (vv. 10–11)

_____

_____

4. What do Saul's actions in verse 12 tell us about the direction of Saul's heart? _____

_____

5. Is Saul's report to Samuel the truth? (v. 13) _____

_____

6. How does Samuel seek to gently lead Saul to personal responsibility? (vv. 13–15) _____

_____

_____

Listen to
Yourself!

7. What is Saul's response? (Note the pronoun usage.) _____

_____

_____

8. In verses 16–18, why do you think Samuel reminded Saul that it was God who took Saul from being a "nobody" and made a king of him before God asks him the question in verse 19? _____

_____

_____

9. How does Saul confirm that his heart is rebellious? (vv. 20–21)

_____

_____

10. In my Bible, this story is titled "Saul's Incomplete Obedience." What does God call it? (vv. 22–23) How is Saul's perspective different from God's? What are the consequences? _____

_____

_____

_____

11. As Saul finally admits in verse 24 that he has done wrong, what excuse does he give for his sin? Is he taking responsibility for his choices? _____

_____

_____

_____

12. What are the consequences of Saul's rebellion? _____

_____

_____

13. Saul went on the mission as commanded, but he interpreted God's instructions according to what he thought was best. Is there any area of your life in which you "incompletely obey" God, or one in which you just don't listen to Him? _____

_____

_____

_____

_____

_____

_____

Pray. Ask God to search your heart and see if there is any rebellion in you. Accept full responsibility. Repent from your heart.

Praise God for His mercy toward you, that He has not left you. Ask for His grace (that He would give you the desire and power to do His will). Commit to complete obedience in the future.

Digging Deeper:

Proverbs 17:11
Proverbs 29:11
Ephesians 5:6–8
Proverbs 27:4

James 4:1
Deuteronomy 11:26–28
Hebrews 5:8–9
1 Samuel 16:14–23

25 Strive Not!

"Better is a dry morsel, and quietness therewith, than a house full of sacrifices with strife" (Proverbs 17:1).

Read 1 Thessalonians 4:7–12 and Matthew 6:31–34.

Quietness, which is desired by many, feared by others, and elusive to most of us, is apparently very important to God. This verse reveals things that are linked with strife as opposed to peace and quiet. A dry morsel is contrasted with a house full of sacrifices ("feasts" in some translations).

Many of the Jewish sacrifices were times of feasting, often lasting several days. A "house full" implies abundance. There is nothing wrong with sacrifices, feasts, or abundance. God instituted feasts and sacrifices, and the provision of the full house is from God. However, there is a problem when we take God's provision and use it for our own purposes.

The Hebrew word for *quietness* involves more than lack of noise; it implies security and abundance. It includes an inner rest and peace. We are to "follow peace with all men, and holiness, without which no man shall see the Lord" (Heb. 12:14). God wants us to be at peace, resting in Him, trusting Him with our lives. Our own striving will hinder us from experiencing peace and, more importantly, from seeing God.

A house full, with strife, indicates that we are seeking our own pleasures and ambitions. Are we pursuing the feast—the fun, the entertainment, the pleasure? Do we desire the full house—the wealth, the abundance, the material things? Neither the feast nor the full house has the capacity to bring true delight or satisfaction. However, as we seek first God's kingdom and His righteousness, we will be satisfied, and we will not dwell in strife (Matt. 6:33).

If our lives are filled with anger and strife rather than with quietness and peace, we need to stop and ask ourselves what we are seeking. Are we striving to satisfy our own desires, or are we seeking the kingdom

Strive Not!

of God and His righteousness? It is better to have a dry morsel accompanied by quiet, than a house full of abundance and feasts that are accompanied by strife.

Pray: Ask God to forgive you for striving after things to satisfy yourself. Ask God to open your eyes to see the vanity of the temporal and the reward of the eternal, and to give you the grace and strength to seek first His kingdom and His righteousness.

25 Strive Not!

Application of Proverbs 17:1

"Better is a dry morsel, and quietness therewith, than an house full of sacrifices with strife" (Proverbs 17:1).

1. What does James say is the source of our conflicts? _____

_____

2. What label does he give to those who seek things only for their own pleasure and satisfaction? _____

3. How does it affect their relationship with God? _____

Summarize these verses in your own words. _____

_____

_____

_____

_____

Read Proverbs 21:17.

4. What happens when a person loves pleasures? _____

_____

Read Matthew 5:6 and Matthew 5:10.

5. What would God have us seek? _____

_____

6. What reward does God promise? _____

_____

"What is the source of quarrels and conflicts among you? Is not the source your pleasures that wage war in your members? You lust and do not have; so you commit murder. And you are envious and cannot obtain; so you fight and quarrel. You do not have because you do not ask. You ask and do not receive, because you ask with wrong motives, so that you may spend it on your pleasures. You adulteresses, do you not know that friendship with the world is hostility toward God? Therefore whoever wishes to be a friend of the world makes himself an enemy of God" (James 4:1–4, NASB).

123

Strive Not!

Read Galatians 6:7–8.

7. What determines what man receives? _____

_____

Pray: Write out the commitment you would like to make to the Lord in response to what He has spoken to you in the verses above.

_____

_____

_____

_____

Digging Deeper:

Ecclesiastes 2:1

Matthew 19:21–23

1 Timothy 5:6

Romans 14:17–19

Isaiah 32:16–18

Luke 8:14

Romans 8:4–6

26 Hidden Hatred

"Whose hatred is covered by deceit, his wickedness shall be showed before the whole congregation" (Proverbs 26:26).

Read Matthew 5:43–48.

Hatred is a strong word. If we have grown up in Christian circles, we are slow to admit that we might hate someone else, because we learned as children that we should "love our neighbor as ourselves" (Mark 12:31). We deceive ourselves into believing that our aversion and dislike of someone is just a difference in personality, and we pretend we harbor no hard feelings. But that deception increases the likelihood that the hidden sin will come out for others to see, because hatred and deceit are both roots of anger.

If we harbor ill will toward a person, it is impossible to keep it hidden. In Matthew 12:34 Jesus said, "The mouth speaks out of that which fills the heart." We can put a smile on our face and act pleasant for a while, but if hatred lurks in our hearts, it will eventually express itself in words or tone of voice. No matter how hard we try, we can't keep it hidden. According to this proverb, we can expect our anger to erupt at a time when it will be observed by many other people.

We do have another option. If we don't want others to see the extent of our anger, instead of waiting until our wickedness is displayed, we can voluntarily bring our hatred to the light and deal with it. Jesus is the Light of the world, and He said, "He who follows Me shall not walk in the darkness, but shall have the light of life" (John 8:12, NASB).

When we confess our sin to Jesus, He will forgive us. Through His light, the dark, hidden hatred in our heart will be washed clean, and we will have "the light of life" in its place. We no longer will have to struggle to control the anger that is waiting to spew forth from hidden hatred.

Hidden
Hatred

Note: See Lesson 11 for instructions on forgiving others and Lesson 13 to learn how to get rid of bitterness.

Prayer Focus: (1) Ask God to forgive you for any hatred hiding in your heart, and for any attempts to keep it hidden. (2) Forgive the person (people) for any offense(s) they have caused you, and pray that God will bless them with the knowledge of His love. (3) Ask the Lord to shine His light in your heart, revealing anything else that is hidden, and to fill you with His light so that you might bring glory to His name.

26 Hidden Hatred

Application of Matthew 5:43-48

"Whose hatred is covered by deceit, his wickedness shall be showed before the whole congregation" (Proverbs 26:26).

Read 1 John 2:8–12.

1. If we hate those around us, have we put the darkness behind us?

_____

2. What are the consequences of walking in darkness? (vv. 10–11)

_____

_____

3. Is it possible to be walking in darkness and not realize it?

_____

Read 2 Corinthians 4:6–7.

4. Where does the light shine? _____

_____

5. What is the purpose of God's light shining in our hearts? _____

_____

6. Can we make the light shine in our hearts? _____

_____

Read 1 John 1:5–9.

Synonyms for hatred include *abhorrence, loathing, animosity, bitterness, hostility, aversion, dislike, disfavor, revulsion, repugnance.*[6]

7. What/Who is the light? _____

8. If we hide hatred (or any other sin) in our hearts, we lie. How does that compare to deceit? To hypocrisy? _____
_____
_____

9. What are the results of walking in the light? _____
_____

Read 1 John 4:7–8.

10. What/Who is love?_____
_____

11. How is love related to hatred, knowing God, being God's child, and fellowship with God and others?_____
_____
_____

12. Look again at the answers to #7 and #10. God is light, and God is love. How does light help us understand love? _____
_____
_____

Examples: Light is not conditional. The sun shines whether we deserve it or not. It overcomes darkness. It causes growth, reveals colors, warms, causes a shadow when blocked, etc. Likewise, God's love is not conditional. He loves us whether we deserve it or not. His love overcomes darkness, etc.

Pray: Ask God to forgive you for choosing the darkness and resisting His light. Ask Him to fill your heart with His love, that you might have fellowship with Him and with others.

Digging Deeper:

John 1:1–11	John 8:12, 9:5
John 11:9–10	John 12:35–36, 46
Matthew 22:37	Luke 6:27–36
John 13:34–35	John 17:25–26
Romans 12:9–10	Romans 13:8–10
Galatians 5:13–15	Galatians 5:22
Ephesians 4:1–3	Philippians 2:1–5
1 Corinthians 13:1–8	1 Timothy 1:7

27 Trapped!

*". . . Because there were no graves in Egypt, hast thou taken
us away to die in the wilderness? wherefore hast thou dealt
thus with us, to carry us forth out of Egypt?"* (Exodus 14:11).

Read Exodus 14:1–31.

(For the whole story, read Ex. 1–14.)

As the Israelites stood trapped between the army and the Red Sea, they
feared an attack by the Egyptians. Their first response was anger toward Moses. Their fear erased memories of the miracles that had freed
them from Egypt. They didn't see that it was God who had delivered
them. They were angry with Moses and were quick to express it.

The people were afraid because they looked at the circumstances rather
than looking at God. They knew they were doomed, that there was no
way of escape. And they were right; there was no escape—without
God. But they weren't without God; He was right there with them.

There are times in life when we feel trapped or when we've been led
astray. Sometimes we are afraid we'll come to harm if something
doesn't change. When we feel trapped and hopeless, we tend to lash
out at the ones closest to us. Could we be missing the mark? Could we
be blaming a man, when it was God who got us into the situation?

In this chapter, God tells Moses where to camp, that Pharaoh will pursue them, and that the Egyptians will know that He is the Lord. God
was not only not surprised by the turn of events—He initiated them,
and He had purpose!

How often do we look at the circumstances, become fearful, and attack
those around us? If we would look at God and have faith in Him, we
could avoid our anger, see what God is doing, and cooperate with Him.

The difference between the angry mob of Israelites and their peaceful
leader, Moses, is that one is in a place of fear and the other is in a place
of faith. Fear comes from looking at the circumstances; faith comes

Trapped!

from knowing you have a faithful God and looking to Him in the circumstances.

Pray: Ask God's forgiveness for basing your level of faith on the circumstances of life rather than on God's faithfulness in the past. Ask Him to help you keep your focus on Him, and trust in Him when you are afraid.

27 Trapped!
Application of Exodus 14:11

"Because there were no graves in Egypt, hast thou taken us away to die in the wilderness? Wherefore hast thou dealt thus with us, to carry us forth out of Egypt?" (Exodus 14:11).

Israelites: Then they said to Moses, "Is it because there were no graves in Egypt that you have taken us away to die in the wilderness? Why have you dealt with us in this way, bringing us out of Egypt?" (Ex. 14:11, NASB).

Moses: But Moses said to the people, "Do not fear! Stand by and see the salvation of the LORD which He will accomplish for you today; for the Egyptians whom you have seen today, you will never see them again forever. The LORD will fight for you while you keep silent" (Ex. 14:13–14, NASB).

Notice the difference in the response to danger. The Israelites showed fear (v. 11), but Moses was full of faith and expectation (vv. 13–14).

	Israelites (fear)	Moses (faith)
Heart attitude:	Fear, blaming, murmuring	Faith, hope, expectation
	Questioning	Peaceful
Point of focus:	Circumstances	God
Hope for rescue:	Themselves	God
Nature of victory:	Defeat, death	Victory, "never again"

1. How can you tell that God was not surprised by Israel's circumstances? (Read Exodus 14.) _____

_____

_____

_____

Trapped!

"So then faith cometh by hearing, and hearing by the word of God"
(Rom. 10:17).

2. Why is it important for Israel (and us) to "stand by" (stand still and watch) to "see the salvation of the Lord"? _____
_____
_____

3. In what circumstances do you find yourself fearful? Do you tend to blame others? _____
_____

4. In what circumstances is it difficult for you to stand still and wait expectantly on God? _____
_____

5. When you fight your own fights, rather than leave them to God, are they settled forever? _____

6. The next time you are fearful, how do you want to respond? Like Israel? Or Moses? _____

Pray: Talk to God about your fears, your failure to trust Him in the midst of them, and your commitment for the future. Seek Him for His grace to respond in faith.

Memorize Scriptures that build your faith, and meditate on them throughout the day.

Digging Deeper:

Matthew 10:28	Romans 10:17
2 Chronicles 20:1–30	Psalm 118:5–9, 14
Psalm 56:1–4	Psalm 23:1, 4
Proverbs 29:25	Proverbs 3:25–26
Proverbs 1:33	

28 Fret Not!

"Fret not thyself because of evildoers, neither be thou envious against the workers of iniquity" (Psalm 37:1).

Read Psalm 37:1–11.

At times we justify our anger, calling it righteous anger, because we are angry about evil. After all, we're being angry at the things God's angry about! But it isn't that simple. God says clearly not to be angry because of evildoers!

Our anger isn't righteous, because our fretting is contaminated. We see evidence of contamination in the warning to not be "envious against the workers of iniquity." We aren't aware of deceit, but God, who knows our hearts, says that sometimes our anger is from jealousy. Therefore, our anger doesn't represent the righteous anger of God.

We are jealous that the evildoers get away with doing evil. We try hard to do what is right, while they get away with blatant wrongdoing. They often seem to be blessed in their wrongdoing and in their influence on others to do evil.

If we are honest with ourselves, we would admit that there are times when we are envious because the wicked seem to get away with things we wish we could do! Whether we want to join them or not, God clearly says not to fret, stew, or be angry because of those who do evil.

God's ways are different than ours. When we trust Him and wait on Him, the victory is sure. When we launch a personal campaign to right the wrong, it leads only to fretting—and it delays God's final victory.

When forced to deal with the actions of evildoers, our responsibility is clear; we are to fret not. Instead, we are to trust and delight in the Lord, to commit our way to Him and rest in Him (Ps. 37:3–5). If we attempt to fret not, without following through on the admonitions to trust and delight in God, we will fail.

Fret means "to grow warm" or "to blaze up with anger, zeal or jealousy."[7]

Fret Not!

The secret is in the Lord. The power is in the Lord. It is only as we look to Him that we will be able to walk righteously in circumstances that trouble us. Only through Him can we avoid fretting and anger. We can find peace as we know that He is able to keep those things that we commit to Him.

Pray: Ask God to forgive you for your anger and for fretting about the evil of others. Ask God to help you delight and trust in Him (even in the midst of an evil attack) and to create in you a pure heart that will reflect His own heart.

28 Fret Not!
Application of Psalm 37:1

Read Psalm 37:1–11 and meditate on what God is saying to you through this passage. Below are some questions to aid you as you meditate on God's Word.

1. The following verbs in Psalm 37:1–11 are directives to us from God. Find them, and consider their significance to you by answering the question for each verb:

(v. 1) *Do not fret.* Why not? _____

(v. 3) *Trust.* In what? _____

Do good. How? _____

Dwell. Where? _____

Cultivate. What? How? _____

(v. 4) *Delight.* In what? To what end? _____

(v. 5) *Commit.* What? To whom? _____
_____

Trust. What is the promise? _____
_____

(v. 7) *Rest and wait.* How? _____
_____

Do not fret. Because of? _____
_____

(v. 8) *Cease and forsake.* What? _____
_____

Do not fret. Leads to what? _____
_____

Fret Not!

(v. 9) *Will inherit*. What land? _____

_____

2. What does God say concerning the evildoers (those who are "causing" our stress)? _____

_____

_____

_____

_____

(In Psalm 37, note verses 1, 9, 10, 12–15, 17, 20, 22, 35–36.)

3. What does God say concerning the righteous (the humble, the blameless, those blessed by him)? _____

_____

_____

_____

_____

_____

_____

(Note verses: 4, 6, 9, 11, 17, 18–19, 22, 23–26, 27–28, 29, 30–33, 34, 37, 39–40.)

Most of the verbs in the list above are based on trust. Our anger comes from our limited vision because we do not see beyond our own concerns. We cannot see God's purposes in allowing the evil to continue. But we can trust His Word. Meditating on these verses will strengthen you to not get angry as you deepen your belief in God's Word and your trust in Him. An antidote for anger is trust in God.

When struggling with anger, read Psalm 37 to build your faith and trust in Him.

Make notes on what is being asked of you in these verses (especially the first 11 verses) and on the promises of God to you. (Notice that the promises are conditional. If you do your part, God promises a reward.)

Pray: Read back through the chapter, praying in response to God as you read.

(God does use people to accomplish His will in overcoming evil. If you feel God has called you to battle evil, do not proceed without first developing a relationship with Him in which you are trusting and delighting in Him. Without that relationship, you will be attacking the evil in your own strength rather than trusting Him to do it.)

Digging Deeper:

Proverbs 23:17
Romans 8:35–39

2 Corinthians 1:9–10
Romans 2:9–13

29 Pride and Hypocrisy

"And he was angry, and would not go in: therefore came his father out, and entreated him. And he answering said to his father, Lo, these many years do I serve thee, neither transgressed I at any time thy commandment: and yet thou never gavest me a kid, that I might make merry with my friends" (Luke 15:28–29).

Read Luke 15:11–32.

The elder son had been moral, faithful, hardworking, obedient, and responsible, but he was angry. A celebration was being thrown for his younger brother, who had shown great irresponsibility, foolishly squandering his inheritance by pursuing pleasure.

We tend to excuse a little anger in someone who seems otherwise virtuous—especially if we are that someone. In this situation, wasn't the elder brother justified? He had been responsible and done what was right, had he not? In contrast, his brother was the perfect picture of self-indulgent irresponsibility and had only reaped what he deserved, right?

It is easy to judge the sins of the younger brother; they are external and visible for all to see. However, the vice of the "virtuous" brother, though hidden, may be a more serious sin in the eyes of God. He had seen himself (and probably, the world had seen him) as a noble son, but the anger he expressed revealed rottenness within his heart.

God looks at the heart. In this one scene of sullen anger, the elder brother shows a heart full of sin. He was jealous, proud, and self-righteous, which led him to judge his brother and his father. These hidden attitudes led to anger, sullenness, and refusal to attend the party.

Before we can point a finger at someone else's shortcomings, no matter how bad or how visible, we need to first deal with the shortcomings in our own life. We are responsible for our own hearts.

Pride and
Hypocrisy

Anger over someone else's sin is usually a clear sign that we are hiding sin under a veneer of pride and self-righteousness. When we deal with our own sin, we have more compassion toward those around us and can rejoice when they turn from sinful ways.

Pray: Ask God to search your heart and reveal your hidden sins. Ask God to forgive you for the sins of hypocrisy, pride, self-righteousness, judgment, anger, etc. as He reveals things to you. Pray for His mercy and blessings on those against whom you have reacted.

29 Pride and Hypocrisy
Application of Luke 15:28-29

"And he was angry, and would not go in . . . . And he answering said to his father, Lo, these many years do I serve thee, neither transgressed I at any time thy commandment: and yet thou never gavest me a kid, that I might make merry with my friends" (Luke 15:28–29).

Read Isaiah 64:6, Romans 3:23, and Matthew 23:27–28.

1. Would the elder brother deserve to be described in the same way Jesus described the scribes and Pharisees? _____

_____

2. What was Jesus' term for someone who seeks to look good on the outside, without concern for the inside? _____

_____

3. We all can probably name others who would fit this description. When is it a description of you? _____

_____

_____

Read Romans 14:12–13.

4. As we judge another person, how does it affect him? _____

_____

5. Could the judgment and anger of the elder brother have been a stumbling block that encouraged the younger brother to leave home? If so, how? _____

_____

Read Philippians 2:1–4.

6. What does God tell us to look for in determining a relationship with others? _____

_____

_____

7. What is that relationship to be like? _____

_____

_____

Read Philippians 2:5–8.

8. How did Jesus demonstrate this truth for us? Is He asking you to do something that He has not done Himself?_____

_____

_____

_____

List the people that you find difficult to relate to. _____

_____

_____

9. Consider Philippians 2:1–8 in relation to these people. What is God asking of you concerning them?_____

_____

_____

Read Ezekiel 36:26, 2 Corinthians 12:9–10, and Revelation 1:5.

10. What does God say He will do? _____

_____

11. Can you be transformed on the inside too? _____

Pray: Cry out to God for forgiveness for your pride, and ask Him to put a new heart within you—a heart that is free from hypocrisy. Rest in Him and the truth that His grace is sufficient.

Digging Deeper:

Proverbs 11:2   Proverbs 13:10

Romans 12:16   2 Samuel 16:7

Proverbs 29:23   Titus 3:5

Matthew 7:2–5   Luke 6:39–45

John 8:3–7   John 15:11–13

Matthew 23:10–12   Philippians 4:8

30 Not My Fault!

"And Jacob's anger was kindled against Rachel: and he said, 'Am I in God's stead, who hath withheld from thee the fruit of the womb?'" (Genesis 30:2).

Read Genesis 27:1–41 and Genesis 29:30–30:2.
(For the full story, also read Genesis 25:21–34 and Genesis 28:1–30:2.)

Rather than being sensitive to Rachel's agonizing cry for children, through his anger Jacob piled more hurt on top of the intense pain she already felt. Could it be that anger was kindled in Jacob because of guilt from his own past actions?

By deception and manipulation Jacob had withheld the blessing due Esau (Gen. 25:27–34). Years later, when Rachel looked to Jacob for the blessing of children, his cutting response would have been an appropriate accusation for his own sin with Esau: "Am I in God's stead, who hath withheld from thee the . . . [blessing]?"

When unresolved sin festers within, it will not die if it is ignored. Instead, it grows and creates guilt, producing disharmony and destruction in relationships. Jacob's unresolved sin led to misplaced anger toward his cherished wife.

When we are angry, we need to look at our own lives rather than looking at the faults and shortcomings of others. Hidden sin breeds more sin. To find freedom, cry out to God, "Search me and know me and see if there is any hidden sin in me" (Ps. 139:23).

We sometimes resolve the immediate conflict without resolving the root from which it sprang. To address the root, deal with the hidden sin. Confess it and take back the ground that has been given to the enemy. As long as the sin is hidden, the enemy has territory from which to stir up anger.

God sent His beloved, perfect, sinless Son to carry that sin for us so that we could have fellowship with Him and with one another. But He

Note: See Lesson 13 for directions for taking back ground that you have surrendered to the enemy.

leaves the choice with us: we can carry the guilt, or we can confess our sins and place them on Jesus. Only as we choose openness and cleansing by His blood will we have freedom from anger. Only as we choose life will we have full fellowship with Him and with each other.

Pray: Confess the hypocrisy of condemning the sins of others, but not your own. Ask God to reveal any hidden sin and to teach you to walk with a clean heart, in order to enjoy fellowship with Him and with others.

30 Not My Fault!
Application of Genesis 30:2

"And Jacob's anger was kindled against Rachel: and he said, 'Am I in God's stead, who hath withheld from thee the fruit of the womb' "? (Genesis 30:2).

Note: Genesis 27 gives the background story of Jacob stealing the birthright from Esau.

Read Genesis 30:1–2 and Matthew 7:1–5.

1. What was the beam in Jacob's eye? What was the mote (splinter) in Rachel's eye? _____

_____

2. When have you been angry with someone else because of a beam in your own eye? _____

_____

3. What does God call people who judge others when they are guilty themselves? _____

4. What does He instruct us to do? _____

_____

Read 1 John 1:5–9.

5. If we hide sin in our hearts, what does it do to our relationship with God? _____

With others? _____

6. Do you want to be free of anger and walk in fellowship with God and one another? _____

If your answer is yes, take time to confess those things to God. Make a list of all that He brings to mind. _____

_____

_____

7. Is there something hidden in your heart that is hindering your fellowship and needs to be brought to the light? _____

_____

Pray through each item in #6 and #7, one at a time, confessing your sin and asking for forgiveness.

Read James 5:16.

Sometimes it is necessary to confess to a brother/sister in order to gain freedom from the hold the sins have on our lives. If you do not experience freedom, seek out a godly person who can hear your confession to God and can pray with you.

"If we confess our sins, he is faithful and just to forgive us our sins, and to cleanse us from all unrighteousness" (1 John 1:9).

Pray: Summarize what God has spoken to you, or write a prayer to Him.

Digging Deeper:

Isaiah 2:5   Psalm 32:5
1 Kings 8:34–36   Matthew 15:18–20
Psalm 37:5–6   John 12:35
Isaiah 5:20–21   Matthew 6:22–23
James 1:19–24

31 The Battle of Lust

"What is the source of quarrels and conflicts among you? Is not the source your pleasures that wage war in your members?" (James 4:1, NASB).

Read Matthew 5:27–29 and James 4:1–4.

A battle of immorality rages in the world today. We are accosted by the lures of sin at every turn. However, God says that the real battle is waged in our hearts, as we decide individually whether to give in to our lustful pleasures or to keep our hearts pure.

Jesus said that everyone who looks on another with lust has committed adultery already in his heart and that we should get rid of the eye that makes us stumble (Matt. 5:28–29). That's radical. Jesus didn't tell us to rid the world of the evil that seeks to trap us. He put the responsibility on us to maintain a pure heart. Each of us is responsible for our own heart.

Difficult people and circumstances don't cause anger. Quarrels and conflicts spring from the battle for pleasures within our hearts. Whether it is a man lusting after a woman, a woman longing to be cherished by a man, someone lusting for unnatural fulfillment, or for fulfillment in other areas, if we long for something that we cannot righteously have, the heart becomes a battleground.

When we allow the conflict to continue, we ally ourselves with the world and become hostile toward God (Jas. 4:4). Through lusting after pleasures, we give Satan a piece of our soul on which to build strongholds. From those strongholds he seeks to destroy us by filling our hearts with anger, fears, anxieties, greater lust, and so forth. If we fulfill our desires outside the boundaries set by God, we will continue to struggle with anger.

To gain freedom from anger, we need to deal with the lusts that war within our souls. God's grace is sufficient to give us strength to deny the pleasures that entice us. We cannot serve two masters at the same time. We can choose self-serving lust, or we can choose to follow God. He will show us the path to freedom.

Pray: Ask God to search for any immorality that is lurking in your heart. Confess failures and unlawful desires. Ask His Spirit to work in you as you seek to gain freedom from the battle that rages.

31 The Battle of Lust

Application of James 4:1

"What is the source of quarrels and conflicts among you? Is not the source your pleasures that wage war in your members?" (James 4:1).

Note: Guidelines to gain victory are given below, but life and freedom will be obtained only to the degree that you apply these truths to your life. If you are serious about gaining freedom from anger, take time to bare your heart before God. Be open and honest. Be specific concerning sins, situations, and people. If this has been a problem area for you, open your heart to someone who is spiritually mature so he or she can pray with you for freedom.

Read James 4:1–12 and follow the steps to freedom that are outlined in these verses.

1. Ask God's Spirit to dwell in you, bring conviction, and lead you to freedom. (v. 5)

2. Submit to God. (v. 7) Admit your failure, need, and willingness to submit to:

    ✳ His leadership—as you trust Him to do His will in your life.

    ✳ His standards for purity.

3. Resist the devil. (v. 7) Reject illegal desires of your flesh and the devil's lures that draw you.

4. Draw near to God. (v. 8) It is only through God's power and strength that you will gain victory.

Incomplete repentance will block complete victory. If you are not grieving over your sin, you have not yet seen it from God's perspective. Study the Bible to gain God's perspective.

5. Cleanse your hands. (v. 8) Repent and turn from the thing(s) God is convicting you of. Get rid of any item (pictures, gifts, trinkets, etc.) that can remind you of a person or an event that is connected to a strong temptation or a time in which you stumbled.

6. Purify your heart. (v. 8) Sinful actions proceed from sins of the heart. Confess your sins and seek God's forgiveness, or you will remain double-minded and fall back into sin.

7. Be miserable, mourn, and weep. (v. 9) Repent and grieve over your sinful actions and heart.

8. Humble yourself. (v. 10) Confess your sins to someone who will hold you accountable to God's standards. God is opposed to the proud but gives grace to the humble. (v. 6)

   If you are judging another person, you have not yet seen the judgment that is rightfully yours.

9. Ask God's Spirit to dwell within you and to guide you in the days to come. (v. 5)

Digging Deeper:

Psalm 14:2–5
Matthew 11:12
Colossians 3:1–14

Matthew 6:24
Romans 7:17–8:13
1 Corinthians 6:9–11

End Notes

1. Strong, James, *The Exhaustive Concordance of the Bible: Dictionaries of the Hebrew and Greek Words,* MacDonald Publishing Company, McLean, Virginia, 1890.

2. Ibid.

3. Ibid.

4. Ibid.

5. Ibid.

6. Rodale, J. I., *The Synonym Finder,* Warner Books, Inc., New York, New York, 1986.

7. Strong, James, *The Exhaustive Concordance of the Bible: Dictionaries of the Hebrew and Greek Words,* MacDonald Publishing Company, McLean, Virginia, 1890.

In Closing: Run the Race

"Trust in the LORD with all thine heart: and lean not unto thine own understanding. In all thy ways acknowledge him, and he shall direct thy paths" (Prov 3:5–6).

Congratulations on finishing the course! I trust that you are now experiencing freedom from the bondage of anger. Be forewarned, however, that the enemy will continue to attack. Completing *Uprooting Anger* does not guarantee an anger-free future. Satan will seek every opportunity to steal your joy, destroy relationships, and discredit your testimony through anger.

However, you do not have to live in bondage to anger. You now have tools to resist the enemy. You know to stop and ask the Lord to identify the root of anger in any particular situation. You now understand how to clear your conscience, to ask forgiveness of the person you offended, and to regain ground given to the enemy through bitterness or other sin. As you maintain diligence in attacking the roots of anger, you will overcome anger in your life.

Uprooting Anger did not cover all the verses on anger. But God knows your heart. Remaining free from anger does not depend on your knowledge. Any time you become angry, ask God to reveal the root to you—then deal with it quickly.

My husband, Robert, had a terrible anger problem. He worked hard to manage it, only to learn it had become worse than ever. In despair he cried out to God to either kill him or take away his anger. God told him, "Quit trying to control your anger, and learn to love." He realized that the more he focused on not being angry, the angrier he got—and that he didn't have genuine love for others.

As he cried out to God to teach him to love, God transformed his heart. As his love increased, his anger decreased. Miraculously, the Lord freed him from the bondage of anger. It was a gradual process, but Robert is now a new man.

If you are still struggling with anger, don't lose heart. Keep your eyes on Jesus, the author and finisher of your faith. Remember that your sufficiency is in Him. You can overcome through Christ as you allow Him to strengthen you and change your heart, rather than trying to change on your own. Continue to seek Him, and He will transform you. He will never leave you. He has promised to complete the work that He has begun in you. Therefore, be strong in the grace that is in Christ Jesus as you run the race that He has set before you. (See 2 Cor. 12:9, Phil. 4:13, Heb. 13:5–6, Mt. 7:7, Titus 2:14, Phil. 1:6, 2 Tim. 2:1, and Heb. 12:1–2.)

Kay Camenisch

Kay Camenisch wrote the meditations for *Uprooting Anger: Destroying the Monster Within* as she was seeking God for answers for Christian couples she and her husband, Robert, were counseling. The parents were trying to control their anger, walk in righteousness, and raise godly children, but they were failing in their efforts. (They had all called to seek placement for troubled sons in a residential treatment facility.) Anger was undermining their efforts to build godly families.

Kay searched the Bible for answers that showed how to obey God's command to get rid of anger, not just to manage it. *Uprooting Anger: Destroying the Monster Within* resulted from a cry to God to reveal His key to freedom and from a search of Scripture passages that deal with anger. The answers found were different than what she sought.

Photograph by Barbara Ann's Photography

Kay has been in ministry with Robert for over thirty years. Together they have taken courses in ministry and counseling, and have co-labored in personal ministry as Robert pastored churches. They served as missionaries in Brazil and later worked in a Christian school where Robert was the principal. While working for the Institute in Basic Life Principles, Robert and Kay coordinated EQUIP, a program that trains young adults to work with troubled teens. The book developed as a result of a time when they served as directors of a residential treatment center for juvenile delinquents. Learn more about their ministry at www.randkcamenisch.com.

I would like to hear from you.

Please share your comments or testimony at: **Kay@camenisch.net**